About the author

Pádraig Carmody lectures in development geography at Trinity College Dublin, from which he holds both a BA in geography and history and an MSc in geography. He completed his PhD in geography at the University of Minnesota in 1998. Subsequently he taught at the University of Vermont, Dublin City University and St Patrick's College, Drumcondra. He also worked as a policy and research analyst for the Combat Poverty Agency in 2002/03. His research centres on the political economy of globalization in Africa.

THE RISE OF THE BRICS IN AFRICA

THE GEOPOLITICS OF SOUTH–SOUTH RELATIONS

Pádraig Carmody

Zed Books
LONDON | NEW YORK

The Rise of the BRICS in Africa: The geopolitics of South–South relations was first published in 2013 by Zed Books Ltd, 7 Cynthia Street, London N1 9JF, UK and Room 400, 175 Fifth Avenue, New York, NY 10010, USA

www.zedbooks.co.uk

Set in Monotype Plantin and FFKievit by Ewan Smith, London NW5
Index: ed.emery@thefreeuniversity.net
Cover design: www.roguefour.co.uk
Printed and bound in Great Britain by CPI Group (UK) Ltd, Croydon, CR0 4YY

Distributed in the USA exclusively by Palgrave Macmillan, a division of St Martin's Press, LLC, 175 Fifth Avenue, New York, NY 10010, USA

A catalogue record for this book is available from the British Library
Library of Congress Cataloging in Publication Data available

ISBN 978 1 78032 605 4 hb
ISBN 978 1 78032 604 7 pb

CONTENTS

ABBREVIATIONS

ABC	Brazilian Cooperation Agency
AFECG	Anhui Foreign Economic Construction Group
ANC	African National Congress
APEX	Agência Brasileira de Promoção de Exportações e Investimentos (Brazilian Trade and Investment Promotion Agency)
BASIC	Brazil, South Africa, India, China
BEE	Black Economic Empowerment
BNDES	Brazilian National Development Bank
BRIC	Brazil, Russia, India, China
BRICS	Brazil, Russia, India, China, South Africa
CNMC	Chinese Non-Ferrous Metals Corporation
DAC	Development Assistance Committee of the Organisation for Economic Co-operation and Development
DRC	Democratic Republic of the Congo
DTI	Department of Trade and Industry (South Africa)
EPZ	export processing zone
EU	European Union
FDI	foreign direct investment
FPI	foreign portfolio investment
G7	Group of Seven Industrial Countries
G8	Group of Eight
G20	Group of Twenty
GDP	gross domestic product
GFC	global financial crisis
GoI	Government of India
HIV/AIDS	Human Immunodeficiency Virus/Acquired Immunodeficiency Syndrome
IBSA	India, Brazil, South Africa grouping
IMF	International Monetary Fund
IPEA	Institute of Applied Economic Research (Brazil)
JSE	Johannesburg Stock Exchange
MDG	Millennium Development Goals
MFEZ	Multi-Facility Economic Zone

NATO	North Atlantic Treaty Organization
NEPAD	New Partnership for African Development
NFCA	Non-Ferrous Metals Corporation, Africa (subsidiary of CNMC)
NGO	non-governmental organization
OECD	Organisation for Economic Co-operation and Development
OLEx	Odebrecht Logística and Exportação
OPEC	Organization of the Petroleum Exporting Countries
PDP	Productive Development Policy
PPP	purchasing power parity
SA	South Africa
SADC	Southern African Development Community
SAPs	structural adjustment programmes of the World Bank and International Monetary Fund
SENAI	Serviço Nacional de Aprendizagem Industrial
SEZ	special economic zone
SMEs	small and medium-sized enterprises
SOE	state-owned enterprise
SSA	sub-Saharan Africa
SSC	South–South cooperation
TAZARA	Tanzania–Zambia railway, also known as TANZAM
TNC	transnational corporation
UN	United Nations
UNCTAD	United Nations Conference on Trade and Development
UNDP	United Nations Development Programme
UNITA	National Union for the Total Independence of Angola
USA	United States
WTO	World Trade Organization
ZCCM	Zambia Consolidated Copper Mines

ACKNOWLEDGEMENTS

The writing of this book was facilitated by a Senior Research Fellowship from the Irish Research Council, whose support is gratefully acknowledged. The opinions expressed here do not reflect those of the Council. The comments of the referees for Zed Books, Nicola Philips, the journal referees and editorial board of *New Political Economy*, the *European Journal of Development Research*, and a referee for the *Handbook of Land and Water Grabs in Africa*, Jim Glassman, Francis Owusu, Anna Gwiazda, Peadar Kirby, Christopher Clapham, Peter Kragelund, Lisa Richey, Scott Taylor, Jiang Xiqian, Kean Fan Lim, James Sidaway, Stefan Andreasson, Karen Smith, Emma Mawdsley, Peter Rutland, Bill Moseley, David Nally, Matthias vom Hau, James Scott, David Hulme and seminar participants at the University of Kwa-Zulu Natal, Queen's University Belfast, University of Plymouth, University of Manchester, University College Dublin and the University of Amsterdam on parts of the manuscript are gratefully acknowledged. The support of the National Geographic Waitt Grant Programme for fieldwork in Zambia is also gratefully acknowledged, as is the permission of Godfrey Hampwaye and Enock Sakala to draw on our article together as a chapter here. I would also like to thank Richard Duggan for his research assistance on the chapter on Brazil and Martyn Davies and Hannah Eddinger for help and suggestions with sources for the chapters on Russia and Brazil. I also thank my colleagues, academic and technical, and graduate students at TCD for their support and a congenial working environment. Thanks also to Ken Barlow and the other staff at Zed. The usual disclaimers apply.

1 | INTRODUCTION: NEW MODELS OF GLOBALIZATION

Then 2009 saw the end of what was known as the 'Third World': We are now in a new, fast evolving multipolar world economy – in which some developing countries are emerging as economic powers; others are moving towards becoming additional poles of growth; and some are struggling to attain their potential within this new system – where North and South, East and West, are now points on a compass, not economic destinies. (Zoellick 2010)

Trade between developing countries, and between them and the BRICS, is rising twice as fast as world trade. Even more strikingly, while growth has headed south, debt has headed north, the opposite of what happened in the 1970s and 1980s, when poor countries ran up vast debts. Gross public debt in the rich countries is rising, from about 75% of GDP [gross domestic product] at the start of the crisis in 2007 to a forecast 110% by 2015, says the IMF [International Monetary Fund]. Public debt in emerging markets is below 40% of GDP and flat. (Economist 2010a: 69, cited in Sidaway 2012: 54)

It is a commonplace to say that global economics and geopolitics are undergoing a major shift. The global financial crisis (GFC), originating from and centred in the West, and the generally rapid growth of a select group of developing countries, particularly the so-called BRICS powers (Brazil, Russia, India, China and South Africa), are two axes or dimensions of this rebalancing of the global geography of power. While the 'rise of China' has preoccupied Western policy-makers for the last number of decades, a growing number of other non-Western powers are challenging the dominance of the traditional 'Great Powers' in the fields of economics, culture and geopolitics.

Why the BRICS?

The BRIC acronym was originally coined by Jim O'Neill, an analyst at Goldman Sachs bank, in 2001. In 2003 Goldman Sachs produced a report in which they predicted that in less than forty years these countries would catch up with the world's major industrial powers and become 'the engine of new demand growth and spending power' (Wilson and Purushothaman 2003: 2). However, as the opening quotes above intimate, this transition is happening much more quickly than anticipated, facilitated in part by the GFC. By way of example, in real terms China's GDP is 50 per cent bigger, India's more than 30 per cent and Brazil's almost 15 per cent compared to the fourth quarter of 2007 (New York Times 2012). By some estimates, on the other hand, the economies of Japan, Britain and France are smaller than they were then, while those of Germany, the USA and Canada are all less than 5 per cent bigger than they were in 2007.

South Africa's growth performance has been the least impressive among the BRICS, as it experienced recession following the GFC and its average income has fallen from 24 per cent below the world average in 1994 to 33 per cent below in 2010 (Clark 2012). Russia also suffered a substantial economic contraction in 2009, as the economy shrank by 8 per cent, as energy prices fell (World Bank 2013). However, economic growth had been rapid in advance of that and revived to average 4 per cent in subsequent years. Moscow is now home to the greatest concentration of billionaires in any one city: seventy-nine as compared to New York's fifty-eight (Voice of Russia 2011).

Given the very different nature of the economies involved in terms of size, structure and growth performance, there has been some debate about the usefulness and validity of the BRICS concept (see Armijo 2007). However, currently the BRICS grouping accounts for more than 40 per cent of the global population, nearly 30 per cent of the world's land area and almost a quarter of the global economy (BRICS 2012). Even more strikingly, their economies accounted for 55 per cent of global economic growth during 2000–08. According to their ministries of finance, 'the inherent strength of the BRICS emanates from strong domestic demand-based economies in the case of India and Brazil and the significant outward linkages of China and Russia. South Africa benefits from its large resource base and proximity to untapped growth potential of the African continent' (ibid.: 5). Already by 2011 the BRICS had more billionaires than Europe, having added, by themselves, almost 10 per cent to the total number of billionaires worldwide in the space of a year (O'Neill 2011).

The scale of growth in China is particularly impressive. 'By 2010, for example, China's GDP had grown by almost US$4 trillion since 2000 – meaning China has, in fact, created another seven Indias (at its 2001 size), nearly three Italys and more than two Frances', dramatically increasing commodity demand around the world in the process (Moyo 2012: 17). China is now the world's largest consumer of copper, accounting for 41 per cent of global demand. It is also the world's largest consumer of many other minerals and cement. This massive demand arises from the need to fuel its export economy, growing domestic demand, and also the urbanization of the country (Harvey 2011; O'Neill 2011).

Collectively the GDP of the BRIC countries (excluding the recent addition to the group of South Africa) is thought to have grown from US$2.5 trillion (2000) to nearly US$9 trillion now (Moyo 2012), as their trade has expanded worldwide. China is now Africa's and Brazil's single largest trading partner and became that country's biggest foreign direct investor for 2010. Outward foreign direct investment from emerging economies is also growing quickly, more than quadrupling from 1995 to 2005 (UNCTAD 2006, cited in Kragelund and Hampwaye 2012).

The rise of the BRICS is mirrored by the relative decline of 'the West', with the Group of Seven (G7) (USA, Japan, Britain, France, Germany, Canada and the UK) share of global GDP falling from 72 per cent in 2000 to a projected 53 per cent in 2011, according to the International Monetary Fund (Wade 2011), and to less than 40 per cent when adjusted to purchasing power parity (PPP), or what their currencies will actually purchase in their home countries. The 'rich country club' of the Organisation for Economic Co-operation and Development predicts that China will overtake the USA to become the world's largest economy by 2016, and that by 2025 the economies of China and India combined will be bigger than those of the G7 industrial countries (Moulds 2012). This shift is also reflected in trade patterns. The ten biggest Asian exporters, outside of Japan, now send only 36 per cent of their exports to the European Union (EU), the USA and Japan, compared to 46 per cent in 1997 (Wade 2011). These changing economic patterns are also reflected in institutional architectures.

The initial four members of the BRIC group recognized the size and dynamism of their economies and the potential to influence the structure of global governance and began to convene meetings beginning in 2009. South Africa is a more recent addition to the group, joining in 2012, but Jim O'Neill has noted that there are other developing countries with bigger economies and better performance than South Africa's, such as Indonesia or Turkey (BBC 2011, in World Bank and IPEA 2011), or Saudi Arabia, which has traditionally been a very important provider of overseas development assistance (Mawdsley 2012).

South Africa's GDP is only one sixteenth that of China. However, it is symbolically, strategically and economically important as it serves as an entry point to the rest of Africa, and is that continent's largest economy. One Brazilian analyst has referred to South Africa as the catalyst for African development and the country is viewed by many multinationals as a gateway or stepping stone to the rest of Africa. For example, Brazilian mining giant Vale has set up an office in Sandton, Johannesburg, as a base from which to pursue its interest in mining and minerals exploration and extraction in Africa (Davies n.d.). South Africa is of substantial strategic importance, as will be discussed in more detail later, and consequently arguably warrants inclusion in the BRICS grouping. Despite only having the 29th-largest economy in the world, South Africa ranks 9th in the index of government economic power (Basu et al. 2011).

Some have also questioned Russia's inclusion in the grouping. It is arguably not a developing country, unlike the other members of the BRICS grouping, with a per capita income of about US$20,000[1] (World Bank 2013). However, it is worthy of inclusion in the grouping because of the size of its economy, which is slightly larger than India's, and its rapid growth. It is now Europe's largest car market (O'Neill 2011). Until the 1990s it had a socialist economic system and consequently it is also worthy of inclusion in this group of substantial or major 'emerging economies'. BRICS nations held five of the top ten spots in the global index of government power in 2009, while older industrial powers, led by the USA, held the other five.

The BRICS grouping finds institutional expression through their annual meetings and also potentially through the creation of permanent institutions, such as the BRICS development bank, which is currently under active discussion. Using a variable geometry, they also coordinate policy positions in relation to issues such as climate change in other fora, sometimes to the chagrin of Western officials (Wade 2011). Each of the BRICS is also the most important and influential regional power in its respective world region: Africa, East and South Asia, Latin America and eastern Europe and the Caucasus. This regional power is expressed in a variety of ways, ranging from Russia's military engagement in the Caucasus, through to influence in institutions such as the newly founded Banco del Sur (Bank of the South) in Latin America or UNASUL (Union of South American Nations) for Brazil. There is also a symbiosis between regional power and global influence which the BRICS cooperation mechanism seeks to crystallize.

Globalization, translocalization and the rise of the BRICS in Africa

The rise of the BRICS is fundamentally reshaping global governance and geopolitics, and also the prospects for African development. During the 1980s and 1990s (and even today) most African countries had programmes with the World Bank and the IMF. These programmes follow the tenets of the so-called 'Washington Consensus' based on privatization and liberalization and were one of the primary modalities through which globalization was facilitated and transmitted to Africa. However, the hegemony of the Western-dominated financial institutions in Africa has been challenged by the rise of the BRICS, recasting the nature of, and differentiating, globalization. For example, the Chinese EXIM (export-import) bank is now the largest provider of loans to Africa, ahead of the World Bank.

The Chinese government is much less prescriptive about the types of economic policies it expects 'client' or 'partner' states to pursue, as long as they remain open to Chinese trade and investment, exercising influence without conditionality (Shinn and Eisenman 2012).

This 'flexeconomy' approach means that the governance templates designed in Washington, DC, by the World Bank and the IMF are now operationalized in a different context. Indeed, with new and emerging alternative sources of finance there is often less pressure to adopt or implement them. This raises the issue of how to conceptualize the impact of these power shifts on the nature of globalization on the continent.

The term globalization is often taken to imply a process of homogenization. Arguably some support could be offered for this proposition, at least in relation to the content of economic policy, during the era of World Bank/IMF 'structural adjustment' in Africa in the 1980s and 1990s when the majority of countries were forced to rapidly implement very similar free market economic reforms – so-called 'shock therapy'. The effect of these policies was to spread and deepen the law of value, or commodification, in Africa, where social relations are increasingly organized on the basis of profit and market exchange. However, the rise of the BRICS has presented African countries with an alternative range of 'partners'; opening up policy space and reconfiguring and restructuring processes of globalization. This conjuncture opens up the potential for African states to play a greater role in the development process, including through welfare programmes which may partially decommodify labour (Esping-Andersen 1990), as have been rolled out in South Africa in particular in recent years (Marais 2010).

There are many different definitions of what constitutes 'globalization'. A 'bare bones' definition is that of an increasing interconnection between places based on greater flows of trade, investment, aid, technology, people and ideas, and perhaps political processes such as electoral democracy (Taylor 2012). However, it could be argued that this definition has an 'inclusionary bias' (Bair and Werner 2011), to the neglect of places that are (being) disconnected along various axes.

Other theorists have taken different approaches to understanding the changing nature of increasingly distantiated social relations. For example, Robertson (1997) preferred the term 'glocalization', which he took to mean the simultaneity – the co-presence – of both universalizing and particularizing tendencies. In its original usage this term referred to the twin processes of the space of circulation of capital becoming global, while the regulation of the 'production-consumption nexus' became downscaled or localized (Swyngedouw 1997). While these ideas offer insight, they arguably do not now adequately capture the evolving nature of globalization in Africa, where many places are becoming more connected, but the precise nature and impacts of these connections vary from location to location based on the types of places from which flows originate and their nature: that is to say that the universalizing tendencies under the current round of restructuring are now less clear and in need of empirical examination. Furthermore, the role of central states in influencing the nature of national development would appear to be increasing, largely arising out of changed power configurations associated with the rise of the BRICS.

The nature of flows between places and countries is heavily influenced by their economic structures. Declining rates of profit in the core industrial economies in the 1970s drove a push to open up markets around the world (Shutt 2009). These states sought to export manufactures and high-value services, in particular, while continuing to import cheap raw materials and also energy. However, the economic structures of the BRICS economies are highly differentiated, which, in turn, results in different types of flows originating from them.

Table 1.1 heuristically captures some of these dynamics. It is heuristic because the content of terms such as 'major geopolitical engagement' can be debated. For example, in the 1970s the Chinese government constructed the Tanzania–Zambia (TAZARA) railway to enable some of the 'Front Line States' bordering or in the same region as apartheid South Africa to circumvent having to export through that country, in addition to supporting a number of 'liberation' movements on the continent.[2] The predecessor state of the current Russian Federation, the Soviet Union, was heavily involved in African geopolitics during the Cold War, as was South Africa. On the other hand, Brazilian and Indian engagement with Africa during the post-colonial period was relatively more muted, until recently. Also, while South African exports are heavily concentrated in natural resources, this is not the case in relation to the African continent, as discussed later, and Africa is also a substantial market for Brazilian manufactures.

TABLE 1.1 Nature of flows from the BRICS

	Yes	No
Dependent on natural resource imports	China, India, South Africa (oil and gas)	Russia, Brazil
Requires food imports	Russia	South Africa, Brazil, China, India (but will change for the latter two in the near future)
Global exports concentrated in manufactures	China, India	Russia, Brazil, South Africa
Previous history of major geopolitical involvement with Africa	China, Russia, South Africa	Brazil, India

The differences in the imperatives and the deepening engagement of the BRICS in Africa is consequently perhaps best captured through the idea of translocalization. Translocalization is the process whereby (some) localities in different world regions become more intertwined through flows of capital, labour, ideas, etc. According to Low and Lawrence-Zúniga (2003), territory in the sense of nations and states is now 'disintegrating' into translocality. While this may be overstated, important shifts in the nature of globalization are under way, which are resulting in new forms of (selective) interconnection and 'graduated sovereignties' (Ong 2000), whereby states are no longer the ultimate arbiters of what takes place in (parts of) their territories, if they ever were. So, for example, there are now Chinese special economic zones in Africa developed by companies from particular places, with tax regimes which deviate from national norms, and a mega-project run by a Brazilian corporation, discussed later, which uses Filipino labour, which has also displaced local people – twin places of dispossession and investment (Büscher 2012). As will be explored later, Chinese demand for copper from Zambia and Indian demand for land in Ethiopia heavily influence the nature of development in those countries, and their constituent localities.

On the other hand, 'cookie-cutter' approaches to globalization of economy, as expressed through World Bank/IMF structural adjust-ment programmes (SAPs), are losing influence. The global ideological template of neoliberalism is giving way to greater pragmatism and flexibility in economic policy-making, at least in parts of the devel-oping world, and bilateral interstate relations, between China and African countries, for example, are rising in importance, as are flows from locality to locality. The influence of policy ideas, prescriptions and practices flowing from international financial institutions to states in Africa is waning, while those from China and other BRICS powers is increasing under the current round of global economic restructuring. This is the correlate of greater material flows of goods, finance and services from localities in Africa to localities in the BRICS powers and vice versa. China is now Africa's single largest country trading partner, for example, and exports of goods and services increased in real terms by 70 per cent from 2000 to 2011 in real terms (calculated from World Bank 2013).

Globalization is being reconfigured as certain 'global' institutions, particularly the World Bank and the IMF, lose influence in parts of the global South, while certain nation-states, and the BRICS in particular, rise in power and influence. This trans*national*ization is the correlate of increasing translocalization in terms of trade, aid and investment projects in Africa.

Their different economic structures and ideologies also mean the different BRIC powers have different globalization strategies, explored in more detail later, and consequently also have different types of flows originating from them. Depending on the different structures of their economies, they generate different types of in-vestment flows and their different domestic politics influence their overseas development assistance strategies. What we are witnessing, then, is a more differentiated geography, arising from uneven exter-nalization and grounding of different types of flows, with different imperatives driving them from the different BRICS powers, with domestic social structures also influencing the nature of overseas engagements, elaborated through the example below.

The different BRICS countries have different development profiles, but with some similarities along certain axes. All of the BRICS are classed as 'medium human development' under the United Nations

Human Development Index (Soares de Lima and Hirst 2006; UNDP 2012). All also have high levels of income inequality, although this is particularly pronounced for South Africa and Brazil, which rank 116th and 117th respectively out of 124 countries for the highest levels of income inequality (Flemes 2009). However, while increased inequality would appear to be a universalizing tendency of neoliberal globalization, Brazil has managed to reduce it in recent years based on its particular policy mix (World Bank and IPEA 2011). What the Brazilian experience shows is that an activist public policy can counter the seemingly universalizing tendencies of neoliberal globalization, with important implications for African development. This experience, in turn, informs the country's overseas development assistance as 'Brazil and other emerging countries are eager to emphasize the differences between their "new" approach – which stresses respect for sovereignty, non-interference in domestic affairs, rejection of tied aid, and an emphasis on technical cooperation – and that of traditional North–South cooperation' (ibid.: 103).

While Western 'donors' attempted to coordinate their aid delivery in the 2000s, partly perhaps in response to the perceived challenge from China (Mawdsley 2012), relations between the BRICS in Africa are marked by both competition and cooperation. For example, former Brazilian president Lula spoke of China as a rival on the continent (World Bank and IPEA 2011) and some Chinese companies have taken previously agreed projects away from Brazilian companies, such as the Belinga iron ore mine in Gabon, which Lula had previously lobbied for (Alden 2009). However, they also cooperate, with China and Brazil agreeing to distribute images from the Sino-Brazilian Earth Resources Satellite to Africa for free (Visentini 2010). This co-opetition (Dowling et al. 1996) has changed the nature of governance in Africa, as will be discussed during the book, and these changes take place in the context of a (re-)emergent regional imaginary described below.

The changing governance context: the creation of South Space

[I]t is naïve to think that there is no danger of imperialism from the East. In world power politics the East has as much designs on us as the West and would like us to serve their own interests.

(Jomo Kenyatta, first president of Kenya, 1971, quoted in Mawdsley 2012: 3)

South–South Cooperation (SSC) refers to the exchange of resources, personnel, technology and knowledge between 'developing' countries – a loose definition that can cover almost any form of interaction from South–South foreign direct investment by Asian, African and South American multinational firms ... to diplomatic meetings and agreements, to the provision of technical experts. (ibid.: 63)

What is emerging is a 'World Without the West'. This world rests on a rapid deepening of interconnectivity within the developing world – in flows of goods, money, people and ideas – that is surprisingly autonomous from Western control ... The rising powers have begun to articulate an alternative institutional architecture ... [that] proposes to manage international politics through a neo-Westphalian synthesis comprised of hard-shell states ... Inviolable sovereignty. (Barma et al. 2007: 23–4, 25, 27, quoted in Armijo 2007: 27)

More than twenty years ago, on the basis of drastically different economic performance and divergence, Harris (1986) announced the end of the 'Third World'. Previously the 'Third World' had been defined by export-oriented, commodity-based economies and membership of the Non-Aligned Movement, which supported neither the United States nor the Soviet Union. However, the industrialization of parts of Asia, in particular, disrupted this regional imaginary. Paradoxically, since then the growth of Asia, particularly China and India, and also Brazil, and their search for raw materials, markets and investment opportunities have reinvigorated the discourse around 'the South' and given rise to a modified mega-regional imaginary which I am calling 'South Space'. This is a region defined by history, material flows and purportedly more equal, and less exploitative, social relations than those characteristic of North–South relations.

During diplomatic or state visits by leaders of the BRICS powers to Africa, different discourses are deployed. However, reference is often made to a shared history of colonial exploitation and the importance of 'South–South' cooperation. Together these practices are creating a distinctive regional imaginary.

South Space has a variety of different discursive and material dimensions:

- Intensifying material flows of aid, trade, investment and people.
- As a global region defined by post-coloniality and increasingly harder (more sovereign) political borders.
- It is constructed partly in opposition to perceived US or Western 'hegemonism' or hegemonic tendencies.
- As a region characterized by more equal, horizontal, rather than vertical, economic and political relations characteristic of North–South interactions. One expression of this is 'development co-operation', instead of aid, and 'win-win' interactions. For example, as Tan-Mullins et al. (2010: 861) argue, the terms '"donor" and "aid" are seen as anathema to China's vision of itself'.
- In reality it is open to a variety of influences – cultural, economic and political – from both East and West.

These dimensions will now be dealt with as they apply to Africa in particular.

While world trade tripled between 2000 and 2009, it grew tenfold between the original BRIC countries and Africa, from US$16 billion to US$157 billion (World Bank and IPEA 2011). China is now South Africa's number-one trading partner (Vigevani and Cepaluni 2009), and relations between the BRICS countries and Africa continue to deepen, the GFC notwithstanding. For example, China's trade with Mozambique increased by 42 per cent in the space of roughly a year from 2011 to 2012 (Macauhub 2013). In the case of Brazil, its trade with Africa initially peaked in 2008 at US$26 billion (World Bank and IPEA 2011), but subsequently fell back as commodity prices declined in the wake of the GFC. However, by 2011 it had rebounded to US$28 billion (Ogier 2012). Within sub-Saharan Africa (SSA), South Africa accounts for almost 20 per cent of imports from Brazil, over 80 per cent of which are manufactured goods (Visentini 2010). Nigeria by itself accounts for a third of SSA trade with Brazil. While the intensity of trade within the global South is increasing, it has a differentiated geography in terms of volume and composition. Over 90 per cent of China's exports are manufactured goods, with all of the developmental benefits that implies (BRICS 2012), whereas Africa still exports mostly primary products (Bond 2006b), largely reinscribing a colonial division of labour, although basic manufactured exports, such as processed metals from Africa, have also been growing.

The discursive construction of a homogenized 'South Space' also runs up against some other hard material realities, such as the very uneven resource geography characterizing the global South. For example, despite it having the world's largest population, at around 1.3 billion people, only 12 per cent of China is arable land. Furthermore, arable land is being lost at a rate of around a million hectares a year as the country urbanizes and parts of it suffer land degradation (Moyo 2012). In India, as explored later, the sometimes fragmented pattern of landholding is encouraging agro-conglomerates to invest overseas, in Africa in particular. These, among other reasons, have resulted in massive 'land grabs' across the continent (Pearce 2012). These land grabs have been facilitated by the fact that across much of Africa land ownership is vested in the state.

This is also a virtual water grab, given increasing scarcity associated with this resource. It takes more than six hundred gallons of water to produce one four-ounce beef hamburger (Moyo 2012), and as the availability of natural resources decreases securing access to them has become a priority for emerging powers (Klare 2008). China is also choosing to import coal and zinc, for example, despite having substantial resources of both of these minerals; perhaps as a hedge against anticipated scarcity. Gaining access to land and water resources through power and influence projection to sustain and expand 'national carrying capacity' are becoming increasingly important policy imperatives for a number of emerging powers.

While South Africa, Brazil and Russia are major natural resource exporters, economic growth in China and India, in particular, depends on overseas natural resource access. Economic growth, in turn, in China is a *sine qua non* for the continuation of Chinese Communist Party rule, and the Chinese government has also stoked nationalism as an ideology in order to deflect attention from the current problematic modalities of domestic governance. Thus the current hybrid ideology in China could be characterized as 'national materialism', which has been developed in order to shore up communist rule in China.

China's domestic model of governance thus has impacts and implications elsewhere in the global South and requires a Janus-faced foreign policy, based on assertive 'counter-leadership' to the United States in order to maintain and deepen alliances with other governments in the global South which also seek to bolster their own regimes. This strategy of counter-leadership asserts the importance and inviolability of national sovereignty, seeking to build, deepen and exercise influence through bilateral relations and a 'new multilateralism', such as the BRICS coordination mechanism, which excludes Western powers. The changing geo-economy, based on increased South–South interconnection and interdependence, is also reconfiguring global geopolitics.

According to Wood (2003: 143), 'for the first time in the history of the modern nation state, the world's major powers are not engaged in direct geopolitical and military rivalry. Such rivalry has been effectively displaced by competition in the capitalist manner.' However, the argument of this book is somewhat different. It is that while competition has increasingly taken a geo-economic form, it is also increasingly infused with geopolitics. While direct military confrontation between 'Great Powers' has receded, for the time being at least, aid is geopolitically infused, as are the operation of state-owned corporations which are increasingly important in investment, particularly in the natural resource sector. Furthermore, even ostensibly 'public' or publicly traded companies may have substantial indirect state ownership which influences their modus operandi. These issues will be further elaborated and examined later.

In terms of governance in South Space, according to the Cambridge political scientist Stephen Halper (2010), China's 'market authoritarian' model has great appeal in the developing world. For him it is attractive because it combines the stability of authoritarian rule with the power of the market. By making the West of lesser importance in global affairs, according to Halper, China is effectively 'shrinking the West'. However, it is more complex than that, as developing country governments are not just attracted to the Chinese model because of its inherent characteristics, but because they wish to escape Western domination.

Bessis (2003: 180) has argued that 'Western supremacy in the post-colonial world was extended through the universality "embodied in the single form given it by Europe", a universality that renders the specific developmental needs of Third World states as of secondary importance and to be assumed under the larger project of Western-style modernity' (Nel 2010: 971). For Comaroff and Comaroff (2012), modernity is a 'way of being in the world', which in the Western tradition is defined by an emphasis on the importance of the individual and their rights. On the other hand the alternative being promoted and propounded by China, and to a lesser extent the other BRICS powers, rests largely on the primacy of states' over individual rights. This emphasis on sovereignty and states' rights can be used strategically to deflect attempts at Western intervention. China, in particular, exercises a kind of 'polar power', which draws strength from the historical dominance of the West. This is partly why the alternative model is attractive – it enables a bolstering of 'stateness', while China's success in poverty reduction is an added attraction.

While Russia is arguably no longer part of the Third World, although that region initially emerged in eastern Europe historically through unequal trade with western Europe (Stavrianos 1981), it seeks to achieve strategic advantage in Africa through reference to former support by the Soviet Union for African liberation movements. The rise of the BRICS is dramatically changing global power dynamics and relations and empirically further problematizing the concept of the 'global South'. Nonetheless, ideology is central to the construction and maintenance of South Space.

Halper (2010: 71) also argues that while communism is dead, 'a new contest between Western liberalism and the great eastern autocracies of Russia and China has reinjected ideology into geo-politics'. However, again this oversimplifies current dynamics. It is not necessarily authoritarianism which is attractive to state elites and populations, but a different model of globalization which is more state directed and has been more economically successful. The model of globalization which is being promoted by China, and to a lesser extent the other BRICS powers, has a much more prominent direct role for the state, through state-owned corporations, for example, as explored later. State-owned oil companies, such as the Brazilian company Petrobras, control 75 per cent of the world's oil reserves and production (Moyo 2012), and these have been a primary vector of integration between the countries of the global South.

Another integral part of the discursive construction of South Space is development cooperation. Mawdsley (2012) outlines key dimensions of SSC, which are: 1) a shared experience of colonial exploitation and consequently developing country status; 2) based on this, experience in appropriate technologies of development; 3) a rejection of hierarchy in the international system and an emphasis on respect and sovereignty and non-interference; and finally, 4) an emphasis on 'mutual development' and win-win outcomes, which enables the redemption of honour by African countries as markets and investment opportunities, for example. As she recognizes, however, the danger is that these discourses obscure the creation of new hierarchies and the empirical similarities between SSC and North–South cooperation. Commodification of land, resources and, in certain time-places, labour is a strong imperative in 'SSC'. Nonetheless, it is not the only imperative.

While the willingness of Southern donors to fund sports stadia or presidential palaces, such as those constructed with Chinese aid in Zimbabwe or Sudan, is sometimes seen as evidence of underlying material motives, Mawdsley (ibid.) argues that these should be seen in the context of dignity, solidarity and mutual respect. The philosophy of mutual benefit which inheres, and is sometimes explicitly stated, in SSC represents a different 'moral geography' unencumbered by the relations of 'charity' (ibid.). All states in the international system seek to maximize their power and increase their wealth (Krasner 1985). However, Nel (2010) argues that emerging powers are also driven by the dialogic desire for recognition in the international system of states. In part this is driven by the experience of 'national' humiliation under colonialism.

A certain amount of (governance) disorder may also benefit the BRICS powers in Africa. According to Halper (2010), it is not in China's interest to rehabilitate 'rogue' states as their ostracism by the West provides a competitive advantage to Chinese companies. This could be considered a strategy – which Beijing accused Moscow of during the Cold War – of 'fishing in troubled waters' (Coker 1985). For example, when a military coup in 2003 in the Central African

Republic was roundly condemned by much of the international community, the Chinese government offered an interest-free loan and a state visit. This has implications for the nature of citizenship in African countries, which is a highly contested field (Manby 2009), as the neo-Westphalian bargain being promoted by China and the other BRICS powers may compromise individual rights, although these have also been under attack in the West recently since the events of September 11th 2001 in particular.

China and Russia have both supplied substantial amounts of arms to the genocidal Sudanese government, although it should be noted some European companies also retain operations there. While the Chinese government argues that it maintains a policy of non-interference, arms provision to repressive regimes could be argued to be an extreme form of interference, although this is also undertaken to an even greater degree by the United States (Midford and Soysa 2012). Furthermore, there is enough evidence to suggest that some ruling parties in Africa receive direct support (Shinn and Eisenman 2012).[3]

In addition to substantial increases in SSC, the rising powers have influenced the nature of global governance, which in turn has impacts on international development. Mawdsley explores new development fora and institutions, such as the UN Development Cooperation Forum, and what the changing development landscape means for global geopolitics. Many of these new initiatives are both simultaneously progressive and exclusionary. For example, the fact that the G20, which includes many rising powers, has apparently displaced the G8 as the primary forum for global economic discussion and coordination might be seen as a democratization of the international order. However, this new configuration excludes smaller, less powerful, often impoverished states, while arguably co-opting more powerful developing states into previous configurations of power. Thus there are tensions between reform, co-optation and regression. In another example, when voting rights were redistributed in the World Bank in 2010 it was towards 'dynamic emerging economies only', with Africa's voting rights actually reduced from 5.9 to 5.6 per cent (Wade 2011) – 'the G20ization of the World Bank'. Thus despite the South Space discourse of equality, certain developing countries are being empowered within the international system, as others are being disempowered along different dimensions.

The growing power of certain developing countries in global governance is also reflected in a leaked cable from the highest US official for the G20 process, who said 'it is remarkable how closely coordinated the BASIC [Brazil, South Africa, India, China] group of countries have become in international fora, taking turns to impede US/EU initiatives and playing the US and EU off against each other' (quoted in ibid.: 347). Wade argues that the result of this is that the older powers' defensiveness and emerging powers' rigorous guarding of sovereignty have produced a condition of 'every state for itself' in international fora. Although later he distinguishes between three modes of participation in international fora – hegemonic incorporation, multilateral cooperation and Westphalian assertion – and argues these modes will vary depending on the issue area. Hegemonic incorporation is where there is multilateral agreement, but the script is provided by the hegemon (the United States). As described later, however, the script in Africa is no longer being provided by the USA, if it ever was. Another changing dimension of governmentality and governance in Africa is that media, race and cultural representation are also increasingly important in the changing geopolitical economy.

Cultural political economy and the BRICS

The rise of the BRICS in Africa is also having cultural impacts. Recently certain scholars have developed a 'cultural political economy' approach which disputes the ontological separation of these fields (Jessop and Sum 2006).

China's global economic advances and increasing political influence have been accompanied by overseas cultural projection, with the government allocating US$6.8 billion in 2009 for 'overseas propaganda'. According to the Chinese president in 2012, 'hostile international powers are strengthening their efforts to Westernize and divide us. We must be aware of the seriousness and complexity of the struggles and take powerful measures to prevent and deal with them' (quoted in Jacobs 2012). On the other hand, former US Secretary of State Hillary Clinton has said that her country is involved in an 'information war' globally which it is losing. According to the president of China Central Television, which has facilities and now broadcasts in Africa, 'journalists who think of themselves as professionals instead of as propaganda workers, are making a fundamental mistake about identity' (quoted in ibid.). Although it should also be noted that the USA has the 'Voice of America' radio station which broadcasts around the world.

The salience of race is also a feature of the rise of the BRICS in Africa. During the colonial era, 'when ideologies of civic freedom and equality confronted the realities of imperialism and slavery, the effect was to place a new premium on racism, as a substitute for all the other extra-economic identities that capitalism had displaced ... the result was that a new ideological role was assigned to pseudo-biological conceptions of race, which excluded certain human beings, not simply by law but by nature, from the normal universe of freedom and equality' (Wood 2003: 101). However, by the turn of the millennium the well-known Berkeley sociologist Michael Burawoy (2000) had identified the cultural valorization of post-colonial subjects as a trend. This has now acquired geopolitical significance as Brazil presents itself as a predominantly 'black' country, giving it a 'soft power' advantage in its dealings with Africa.[4] Thus the discourse and social construction of race have changed in its relation to capitalism. This will be discussed later in the chapter on Brazil in particular as this discourse feeds into the discursive construction of a (powerful) 'South Space', in opposition to the 'West'.

The following chapters now analyse the nature of BRICS powers' engagements and impacts in Africa, with a particular focus on governance and on understanding their different globalization strategies. Chapter 2, co-authored with Godfrey Hampwaye and Enock Sakala, examines how China exercises influence in Africa, through a case study of Zambia. While much has been written about the scale of Chinese involvement in Africa in recent years, this chapter, based on fieldwork, attempts to theorize the channels, content and meaning of Chinese power projection through a case study. While China is sometimes accused of engaging in neocolonialism in Africa, by American policy-makers, for example, this chapter argues that we need to conceptualize its modality of power projection and governance at a distance in a different way through the idea of geo-governance.

The next chapter examines South Africa's evolving role on the continent. As noted earlier, South Africa is perhaps a somewhat strange inclusion in the BRICS grouping, but given its weight and influence in Africa's political economy it arguably does warrant inclusion. This chapter explores channels and impacts of South African influence and develops a new trade theory. Whereas conventional economic theory argues that trade, under free market conditions, is universally beneficial, this has not proved to be the case. Unequal trade is a well-known phenomenon in the critical political economy literature. However, as South Africa is an intermediate case between a developed and a developing country, its trade profile with the region is different to that of many other countries. Rather, this chapter argues that the developmental impacts of trade should be assessed based on whether or not it is complementary, competitive, consumptive or extractive.

Chapter 4 examines India's involvement in Africa, utilizing a case study of 'land grabbing' in Ethiopia through the lens of the 'geologics' of such investments. Other contributions have examined the way in which India uses development cooperation flows, technical support and assistance, training and other modalities of engagement on the continent (see contributions in Mawdsley and McCann 2011). Along many dimension or axes India is 'globalisation slipstreaming' in Africa behind China (Carmody 2011b); however, this is not the case in relation to land acquisitions, where the Indian government is now reportedly the biggest investor in land acquisitions worldwide (Land Matrix Database, cited in Provost 2012). More than half of all land being sought after by foreign investors is located in sub-Saharan Africa (Gurara and Birhanu 2012).

While the scale of Chinese land acquisitions on the continent has been substantial, and some argue that this will serve as an insurance policy should food shortage become an issue, the Chinese government has for the moment largely forsworn food exports from Africa, given the political sensitivities which attach to them in a continental context of widespread food insecurity (Shinn and Eisenman 2012). However, the Indian government and companies have not shown the same types of sensitivities or concerns for reasons discussed in the chapter. The impact of these large-scale land acquisitions is to expose local people to increased levels of localized and globalized risk, and sometimes displacement. The political logics of these investments, though, often work to the benefit of incumbent African regimes.

While much has been written about China, India and South Africa's roles on the continent, this is less true of the two other BRICS: Russia and Brazil. As the world's largest energy exporter, Russia has, until recently, had less interest in exploiting African energy reserves. However, as the Russian president, Vladamir Putin, has declared that the point of 'peak oil' has now been passed in Russia – more than half of existing reserves have been exhausted (Harvey 2011) – this is changing. This chapter pays attention to the geopolitical code through which the Russian state views Africa. It argues that its engagement with the continent is largely driven by the priority of reviving Russian national power and competing with the United States. Brazil's rising role on the continent has also recently been noted in the media. Brazil's relations with Africa are perhaps more complex than those of the other BRICS powers, given its particular domestic political economy and the distinctive vision of alter-globalization which arises from that, and the nature of its historical ties with the continent. The ways in which its domestic policies inform its foreign relations arguably mean that the division between domestic and foreign policy is being partially broken down: to create a kind of 'intermestic' policy stance (Manning 1977). However, how the particular vectors of Brazilian policy touch down in locales in Africa varies; informing and shaping a kind of geographic BRIColage.

2 | CHINA: GLOBALIZATION AND THE RISE OF THE STATE?[1]

with Godfrey Hampwaye and Enock Sakala

The rise of the Chinese state

Each of the different BRICS powers pursues different globalization strategies, driven by different domestic imperatives. Based on their different economic structures and political economies, foreign policies vary somewhat between them. Through these strategies they are altering the very nature of globalization, as will be described and detailed below.

According to realists, relations of force structure relations between states. While this may be partially the case, persuasion and influence are becoming increasingly important in interstate relations, and all of the BRICS powers deploy these in their tactics in Africa to varying degrees. The emphasis on influence over force in BRICS foreign policies (with the partial exception of Russia) is a reflection of both relative military weakness compared to the USA, learning from the disastrous US-led invasion of Iraq and genuine feelings of solidarity between countries of the global South. The USA has also learnt from its recent experience of overseas military interventionism, and these dynamics together have resulted in a shift away from hegemony in international relations to different types of geo-governance, explored in more detail below.

The predominant narrative of globalization is that it has led to a decline in the power of the nation-state and an increase in the power of markets. Others note that the power of the state has increased along some dimensions, even as it has lost economic power. Both of these literatures, however, tend to be too reductive by focusing on the national scale. In contrast, this chapter argues that globalization may reconfigure, respatialize and potentially increase the economic and political power of certain states.

There are now extensive literatures of the rise of both China (e.g. Breslin 2007) and its increasing role in Africa (e.g. Brautigam 2009). The ascent of China in the international system is of world historic importance (Arrighi 2007), and the increasing influence of that country in Africa is arguably the most significant development in the post-independence era (Taylor 2009). However, with few exceptions (e.g. Kiely 2008), there has been relatively little reflection about how these developments are reshaping the nature of globalization and the implications of this for state, globalization and international relations theory.

Whether China is a rising power has been debated and analysed in the literature (Chestnut and Johnston 2009). Seventy-three of the 500 largest companies in the world are Chinese, ahead of Japan, and many are state-owned enterprises (SOEs) (CNBC 2012; Nolan 2009). While China's economic development has complex reasons and actors involved in it, such as Township and Village Enterprises, its economic ascent is largely based on, and a reflection of, the power of trans-national corporations (TNCs) (Breslin 2007), which now account for more than half of China's exports (Hart-Landsberg and Burkett 2005).

China has undertaken extensive economic liberalization as part of its accession to the World Trade Organization (WTO), eliminating local content requirements, for example (Kiely 2008). It reduced its average agricultural tariff from 54 to 15 per cent, prompting the Chinese commerce minister to argue that 'not a single member in the WTO history has made such a huge cut [in tariffs] in such a short period of time' (Bello 2009: 97). The power of the Chinese state to regulate transnational flows of trade and investment and TNCs domestically would therefore appear to be in decline, confirming the dominant globalization hypothesis of the decline of the state (e.g. Strange 1996). However, as China is giving up the levers of the developmental state domestically, its efforts to promote 'national' champions, or 'dragon's heads', has gone global through the 'go out' policy officially announced in 2003, two years after China's accession to the WTO (Brautigam 2009). Under this policy, through tax and financial incentives, Chinese companies are encouraged to invest overseas.

Rapid economic growth in China has fuelled demand for natural resources, which are largely sourced through Chinese SOEs, and the imperative of opening up new markets. A quarter of China's exports to developing countries now go to Africa (Standard Bank 2010, in World Bank and IPEA 2011). Chinese outward foreign direct investment (FDI) increased nineteen-fold from 2000 to 2006 (OECD 2008) and is growing most rapidly in Africa (Kaplinsky et al. 2010). Increasing outward FDI by Chinese SOEs means they now appropriate surplus value globally, and consequently the external economic power of the Chinese state has increased. Thus, in the Chinese case at least, the economic reach and power of the state are being externalized or globalized in order to fuel continued private-sector-led economic growth, not necessarily reduced (see Lim 2010 and Gonzales-Vicente 2011). This hypothesis is explored in this chapter through an examination of Chinese relations with the southern African country of Zambia through the lens of geo-governance, elaborated in more detail below, where state power is projected across national boundaries.

While survey research has been conducted on Asian investment in Zambia (Carmody and Hampwaye 2010), this chapter adopts a more in-depth qualitative approach to probe the meaning and content of current and previous Chinese investments, in order to examine the way in which new modes of geo-governance are being constructed.

Globalization and the state

There is now a huge literature on the nature of globalization and its impacts on the state. Globalization is often simply defined as the increased interconnectedness between places in terms of flows of trade, investment and ideas. In the last several decades this increased interconnection around the world has been facilitated by liberal international trade and capital regimes as constitutionalized through the WTO, the European Union and other global and regional institutions and organizations (Gill 2003). In the developing world, in particular, globalization has also been facilitated and speeded by the opening up of economies to trade and investment through World Bank- and IMF-sponsored SAPs; latterly reformed and renamed Poverty Reduction Strategies.

In the literature there are contrasting positions about the construction and impacts of globalization on state power. For example,

Harvey (2005) argues that neoliberalism, or state retraction and an emphasis on market processes in allocative decisions, has become dominant around the world since the 1970s, including in China. Others go farther and write of the 'Westfailure' nation-state system which is unable to deal with the challenges of global environmental degradation and effective financial regulation, among other issues (Strange 1999). However, others dispute the narrative of the decline of the power of nation-states.

While acknowledging that 'in the developing world, economic globalisation has created greater pressures and incentives for cross-national policy convergence', Mosley (2005: 356) argues that 'some room for government autonomy and cross-national policy diversity remains'. Also, in relation to Latin America, Phillips (1998: 7) states that 'although the policy autonomy of the state is reduced in terms of the available feasible options, the strength or "power" of the state is enhanced as a result of engagement with processes of international change and its specific manifestations'. Yet others, such as Weiss (1998), argue that there has been much variation in state responses and adaptability to globalization, leading to the emergence of 'catalytic states' capable of shaping globalization to national advantage in certain world regions, such as East Asia.

Specifically in relation to the internationalization of the state, Glassman (1999: 673) defines it as 'a process in which the state apparatus becomes increasingly oriented towards facilitating capital accumulation for the most internationalised investors, regardless of their nationality'. The extension of this imperative worldwide led Robinson (2002: 215) to argue that there is now a transnational state, which he defines as 'an emerging network that comprises transformed and externally integrated national states, together with the supranational economic and political forums and that has not yet acquired any centralized institutional form'; although it could now be argued that the G20 is something approaching such an institutional form. Shaw (2003) goes farther and argues that there is an emergent Western-centred 'global state' which is able to project its power through institutions such as the United Nations. However, there are also other models of internationalization of the state which have emerged as a result of the dialectics of globalization.

Given the extent of many African countries' economic crises during the 1980s and 1990s, and the small average size of their economies, there has arguably been less scope for policy autonomy from the World Bank and the IMF than in many other parts of the developing world. As a result of SAPs, sub-Saharan Africa is now the region of the world most open to trade, with average tariff rates of only 10 per cent (Lines 2008).

According to Hampwaye and Rogerson (2010: 387), 'sub-Saharan Africa during the past two decades has been impacted greatly by decentralisation and globalisation which together reduced central state control of economic development'. However, the argument of this chapter is that there has been an evolution of this, as the state does now seem to be playing an increasingly important role in economic development, in Zambia at least, although the state in question is primarily the Chinese state, rather than the Zambian one. This is not to assume that the Zambian state is 'weak' or 'powerless' or that 'African states are [simply] acted upon: they have a measure of agency in this relationship' (Youde 2007: 4).[2] The claim is not made that the form of geo-governance being constructed in Zambia is being generalized across the African continent, but the case study presented here is suggestive and illustrative of how this new form of power and coordination works.

Chinese geo-governance

In the mid-1990s, the well-known Princeton academic Richard Falk (1995) argued that as a result of the rise of global finance and the increased importance of information and communication techno-logy, the role of the state in international relations was declining and that a new regime of networked geo-governance was emerging. Geo-governance refers to 'the ways in which effective coordination is affected in a world where resources, knowledge, and power are distributed through geographical space' (Paquet 1996: 3). For Paquet, the new model of global geo-governance represented a 'dispersive revolution' as the role of private and non-state actors increased. Others have also noted the growing role of private authority in global governance, where transnational capital exercises indirect, but effective, control over the parameters of many governments' economic policies through the operation of the bond market, among other mechanisms (Hall and Biersteker 2002). However, globalization is dialectical and consequently generates counter-tendencies and other models of governance. For example, in Africa the Chinese state increasingly operates a policy of flexigemony; of working through existing institutions to achieve resource and market access rather than seeking to transform them (see Carmody and Taylor 2010). In contrast to the authoritarianism of conditionality-based SAPs, this mode of governance[3] projected over distance (hence 'geo') represents consent informed by coercion[4] – a kind of 'dethority' exercised through influence, backed by economic force, rather than hierarchical diktat. The Chinese government famously, in theory at least, operates its foreign policy with 'no political strings attached'.[5] This policy finds traction among African political elites as a result of the contrast with the conditionality-based neoliberal mode of geo-governance, with which it now competes and hybridizes.

There is a substantial debate in the literature on the extent to which the Chinese government strategy of economic and political engagement in Africa is planned. Taylor (2009) argues that there is no grand, coordinated strategy of Chinese engagement in Africa, whereas Brautigam (2009: 78) argues that 'Beijing's engagement with Africa involved a well-thought-out and long-term strategy, not the hasty, desperate scramble familiar from the media headlines'. Others see coherence to different axes of engagement driven by structural imperatives (Carmody and Owusu 2007).

While businesses around the world are connected to states through purchasing, taxes and incentives, Chinese business engagement in Africa is different as 'much of Chinese foreign direct investment [FDI] into Sub-Saharan Africa comes from wholly or partially state-owned firms with access to very low-cost capital, and operating with much longer time-horizons' (Kaplinsky et al. 2010: 396). This is particularly significant as Chinese FDI into Africa is growing faster than to any other world region.

In an insightful article, Gill and Reilly (2007: 38–9) outline 'a powerful "principal-agent" dilemma: an increasing set of tensions and contradictions between the interests and aims of government principals – the bureaucracies based in Beijing tasked with advancing

China's overall national interests – and the aims and interests of ostensible agents – the companies and businesspersons operating on the ground in Africa'. They detail how the Chinese central government does not have direct operational control over state-owned and provincial-state-owned corporations operating in Africa, even if they have vested ownership. This is partly as a result of the partial privatization of many SOEs in China (see Qi et al. 2000). Furthermore, Gill and Reilly argue that given the increasingly diverse array of Chinese agencies and actors involved, effective coordination becomes much more difficult. However, while this is an important and interesting exposition, it is not based on empirical research and neglects the informal operation of power and influence which may be at play. For example, it is well known that many 'private' companies in China have Communist Party groups which meet in them, giving the central state insight into and influence over their operations.

On the basis that actions speak louder than words, this chapter adopts a different approach to look at the on-the-ground nature of Chinese socio-economic engagements in Zambia. This is done to assess the way in which new modes of geo-governance are being constructed through economic and political nodes to form a network or matrix of influence and engagement in the country. In particular, it argues for the informal operation of power, and on the basis of the empirical evidence suggests that engagement is structurally coherent and planned, rather than ad hoc or haphazard, with important implications for the globalization theory.

Historical geographies of power: Chinese engagement in Zambia

There is a long history of Chinese politico-economic engagement in Africa, and in Zambia in particular. All of Zambia's post-independence presidents have referred to Zambia's 'all-weather' friendship with China, and it was Zambia which co-sponsored the resolution in the UN General Assembly to restore China's seat on that organization's Security Council (Mutesa 2010). This 'all-weather' friendship has also been referred to by the current president, Michael Sata (Hu and Wei 2011), who had before a previous election spouted virulent anti-Chinese rhetoric about the country needing 'investors not infestors'.

China and Zambia's 'all-weather' friendship found concrete expression in the construction of the TAZARA or TANZAM railway, which was completed ahead of schedule in the 1970s. This railway line links Dar es Salaam, in Tanzania, to Kapiri-Mposhi, in central Zambia, and was built to facilitate Zambian copper exports following the closure of the traditional southern route as a result of sanctions on South Africa and Southern Rhodesia (McGreal 2007; Hampwaye 2008; see Figure 2.1). Geopolitically, it was spurred by the fact that during the 1960s and 1970s, the Chinese state was competing with the Soviet Union for support in Africa (Meredith 2005).

More recently, China has forgiven some of the debts associated with the construction of this railway, arguably for geo-economic, rather than geopolitical, reasons. As China is now the world's largest consumer of copper, it is anxious to cultivate good relations with the Zambian government and thereby secure access to this major local resource.[6] However, this also fits with a broader programme of debt relief to 'highly indebted poor countries', many of which are in Africa, for combined humanitarian, political and economic reasons (Xinhua 2010). The Chinese also built a 1,700-kilometre-long pipeline to bring oil from Tanzania to Zambia in 1968 (see Figure 2.1). While these two projects emphasized movement of goods and people, more recent Chinese projects are at specific nodal sites, showing a deepening level of engagement.

The TAZARA railway was both a practical and a symbolic rejection of the colonial and apartheid regional geo-economy, while also replicating its infrastructural pattern by running from the interior to the coast, rather than developing an internally articulated transport system.[7] In addition to the railway, the TAZARA established a long-lived Chinese business engagement in Zambia. On the outskirts of Lusaka, the Chinese workers who built the TAZARA lived in a compound. In order to build a perimeter wall around the camp to protect the tractors and other construction equipment, a cement block factory was built, which is still in existence. According to a current Chinese manager there, there were 'thousands of machines, like tractors and trucks', some of which are still used to deliver concrete blocks and others of which are rusting in the compound.[8]

While geopolitics and facilitating the movement of goods was the

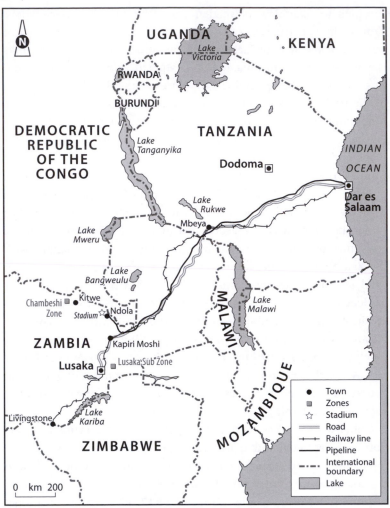

2.1 Selected Chinese-built projects in Zambia

motive for early Chinese engagement in Zambia, deeper geographical embedding at specific nodal network sites through which power can be projected is now more prominent for economic reasons.[9] Thus the geographical infrastructure through which the Chinese state projects its power or liminal and expanding sovereignty in Zambia is undergoing a round of restructuring as reflected in the evolving economic landscape (Harrison 2004). Like the TAZARA, these new sites serve both symbolic and practical functions to achieve a particular type of geo-governance.

While it is only in the last few years that China's increased economic engagement with Africa has attracted substantial media and academic attention, 1997 was a key year for Chinese engagement in Zambia. It is often suggested, by Tony Blair (2008), for example, that China has come from 'under the radar' to become the most influential country in Africa. However, the foundations and groundwork for this were being laid during the 1990s, when China's 'go out' policy to promote its large state-owned corporations, in particular, to expand overseas was enacted, although it was not officially announced until 2003. The *problematique* for the Chinese state in Zambia is how to achieve a conducive investment, market and resource access regime for its companies in the context of often despotic labour practices.

In the 1980s the Chinese had built a major textile factory in Kabwe (McGreal 2007). This was initially intended as a turnkey or build-and-transfer facility to be turned over to the Zambian government, but when it ran into operational difficulties, the Chinese premier suggested it should be run as a Chinese–Zambian joint venture, from 1997, which it subsequently was. However, it could not compete with imports from China and the region and was closed in the mid-2000s with the loss of several thousand jobs directly and of income for thousands of cotton growers (Brautigam 2009; Carmody 2010). This shows that the 'Chinese march into Africa' is not immutable or infallible. However, another node of economic engagement was established in 1997 which, although lower profile, may prove to be more influential and long lived.

A less obvious geographical expression of Chinese economic power was the fact that 'the state-owned Bank of China was directed to set up a branch office in Zambia in 1997 ... to make it easier for Chinese companies to enter unfamiliar territory' (Brautigam 2009: 82). According to a Chinese entrepreneur who had been in Zambia for nine years, the setting up of the bank branch was one of the key reasons she migrated, in addition to the fact that she already had Chinese friends living in Zambia.[10] The fact that there was a Bank of China branch convinced her that Zambia 'should be a safe place', and she along with many other Chinese business people utilize the bank services.

The bank's assets have grown rapidly during that time. For example, its total assets in Zambia increased from 14 billion kwacha in 1997 to 507 billion (US$108 million) in 2008 (Zambanker Reporter 2008), which still, however, represents a small percentage of the Zambian market.[11] According to Kragelund (2009a), the Bank of China facilitates overseas foreign direct investment by Chinese companies in Zambia by offering low-interest-rate loans and, according to an official at the Ministry of Industry and Commerce, it provides finance for Chinese companies in Zambia, most of which are SOEs.[12]

There is still only one small branch of the bank in Zambia with a few counters, which has recently moved from the city centre to an inner suburb.[13] Despite its small physical size, the Bank of China is an important site in mental maps of Zambia for Chinese entrepreneurs; an anchor site of engagement and practical economic support. In addition, in order to encourage further Chinese investment in Zambia, the Chinese Ministry of Commerce instructed that a China Centre for Investment Promotion and Trade be set up in the capital city, Lusaka (Kragelund 2009b).

Despite its rapid growth in Zambia, loans and advances from the Bank of China in the country remained at only 4 per cent of total assets, as compared to an industry average of 45 per cent, raising questions about what the rest of the bank's assets are; probably either in Zambian government bills (debt) or deposits in foreign affiliates.[14] A trade union official noted that 'some investors don't even bank money here' and that Zambia was just used as a transit point for capital.[15]

The Chambishi Multi-Facility Economic Zone (MFEZ) and its impacts on governance

Zambia is now the third-largest recipient of Chinese foreign direct investment in Africa and nineteenth in the world (UNCTAD 2007). In 2007, China invested ten times more than the second-, third- and fourth- largest investors combined (South Africa, Singapore and Great Britain) (Kragelund 2009a), and, according to a manager at the Zambian Development Agency, he would 'never have believed' that an inflow of US$1.3 billion in foreign investment in 2007 could be achieved in the country.[16] Some of this investment is flowing into the new Chinese-built and -run special economic zone (SEZ) or MFEZ in the north of Zambia.

In 2006, the government of China announced that it would support up to fifty overseas 'economic and trade cooperation zones' being set up around the world (Brautigam et al. 2010). In 2007, the Chinese government stated it would provide loans to develop an MFEZ for Chinese and other companies in the Copperbelt town of Chambishi, near Kitwe, in Zambia, with a total targeted investment of US$800 million. These zones serve both economic and political purposes, by contributing to industrialization and facilitating good relations with host-country governments, thereby easing resource access (Carmody and Hampwaye 2010). Given the urgency with which the Zambian government seeks foreign investment, this zone could be seen as an example of Chinese 'flexipower', which combines both a 'hard' economic calculus and a 'soft' socio-political function (Carmody and Taylor 2010).

The Chambishi zone was the first Chinese SEZ to be operative in Africa. According to the Zambian Development Agency MFEZ manager, as of August 2009 there were eight enterprises registered in the Chambishi zone, but only three were operational. Others reported that, as of November 2009, there were eleven companies active there, with another five expected to set up operations shortly thereafter (Brautigam et al. 2010). Of these most are subsidiaries of the developer of the zone, the China Non-Ferrous Metals Corporation (CNMC), and were already there before the zone was announced in 2006. Of the 4,000 workers currently technically employed in the zone, only 600 are actually in the zone, with the majority working in mines or other subsidiaries of CNMC. This has led some to argue that this is in reality a 'pseudo-economic zone' (Michel and Beuret 2009), which is merely designed to lock in tax breaks for Chinese companies in their resource extraction operations. The anchor facility at the zone is a US$250 million copper smelter, which uses ore from the Democratic Republic of the Congo and two mines in Copperbelt Province in Zambia, 'Chip South' and the CNMC mine at Chambishi, which was China's first overseas non-ferrous metals mine, established in 1998.[17] The goal is reportedly to have attracted forty Chinese companies to the zone and ten from other countries by 2011 (Brautigam 2009).

The tax incentives in the zone are graduated, with companies paying no tax in the first five years, 50 per cent of the applicable rate in years 5–8 and 75 per cent in years 9 and 10, after which tax incentives are abolished. In addition, raw materials and capital goods can be imported duty free into the zone. There is some dispute as to whether or not investors in the zone have to be Chinese or not. According to the MFEZ manager at the Zambian Development Agency they can be of any national origin, as long as they meet the benchmark requirement of half a million US dollars of investment in either cash or machinery. However, the Chinese Ministry of Commerce has a contrary opinion (Davies 2008), and it is the Chinese manager of the zone who will decide which companies can invest. According to Kragelund (2009b: 654), 'when all of the investments in the zone have been finalised, the Chinese state – through mostly state owned Chinese companies – will control the full Copper value chain from crushing the rock ... to manufactured copper products'.

Prior to the MFEZ Act of 2006, Zambia had operated export processing zones (EPZs), with the support of the Japanese government[18] (Xinhua 2003). According to Robert, the MFEZ manager at the Zambian Development Agency in 2009, 'the idea of MFEZ is to combine SEZs [operated in China] with EPZs so there is no bias towards exports or selling on the local market ... the emphasis is only on value addition and employment creation'. Rather than trying to engage this foreign direct investment strategically, then, this represents an 'open door' policy whereby companies can have unrestricted access to the local market. However, they can also avail themselves of tax and other incentives, while not being under any obligation to export. This lack of conditions is in stark contrast to the policy pursued in China itself during its industrialization drive (Breslin 2007). According to the MFEZ manager at the Zambian Development Agency, it was 'a bit strategic' in its approach, by targeting Asian countries, particularly China, India and Malaysia, for investment.[19] Even with the global economic downturn there had been 'no slowdown in Chinese investment', and there were trade delegations from Asia asking for 'huge portions of land' for producing exports for the world market. The focus has been on manufacturing, mining and, more recently, on agriculture.[20]

The open door policy is likely to bring relatively few benefits to ordinary Zambians, as it works to the advantage of highly competitive foreign investors with developed technical capabilities and access to low-cost finance. China is able to bring both capabilities and cost to bear, with a Chinese engineer on a one-year project reported to cost almost eight times less than one from Europe, according to one African official (Bilal and Rampa 2011, cited in Mawdsley 2012). In part, it could be argued this is the objective of the zone – to attract foreign investors with higher-level technical capabilities – but this model is enclave-creating. This is reflective of the extent to which liberal economic philosophy has permeated the Zambian state since the implementation of World Bank/IMF programmes in the country in 1993. This philosophy was also in evidence in an interview with some officials from the Ministry of Industry and Commerce who argued that 'any investment is positive'.[21] By inference this might include polluting or highly exploitative industries, such as the Chinese explosives plant in Chambishi, which blew up in 2005, killing forty-nine workers, in what is now the site for the MFEZ. This explosion was perhaps not surprising as the workforce for the plant was selected from casual workers who would gather outside the factory each morning. Needless to say they did not have training in handling explosive materials and the plant was designed for only around twenty rather than fifty workers. The workers did not have to give up their mobile phones, lighters or cigarettes and there were no separate areas for making dynamite and explosives (Michel and Beuret 2009). The company paid less than ten thousand dollars per worker killed to the families. Coincidentally, or not, it was a month after the explosion that the development of the Chinese Special Economic Zone in Chambishi was announced. More broadly, the casualization of labour in the mining industry has been associated with an increase in accidents (Matenga 2009).

There was an acknowledgement by the official at the Ministry of Industry and Commerce that 'back home in China they can give slave wages'.[22] In 2009 the minimum wage was 270,000 kwacha a month in Zambia, but a trade union official reported that in some cases Chinese companies pay only K100,000 a month (about US$22). Such breaches are facilitated through the practice of hiring workers

through labour brokers. However, a manager at Sino-Metals Leach-
ing plant, a subsidiary of the CNMC, which extracts copper from
mine tailings in the MFEZ, insisted that no employee was paid less
than K1 million (US$217) a month, when meal and other allowances
were taken into account.[23] It was further argued that, in addition,
an employee was entitled to a gratuity at the end of each contract
of between one and three years.

Sino-Metals produces only approximately a tenth of the copper
that the copper smelter does and exports 320 tonnes of copper a
year to China to pay off its loans to the state-owned Bank of China,
showing the interlinkages between different state-owned nodes of
engagement. Managers there noted that the fact that their supply
contract with Republic House, the Swiss commodity trading company,
was very stable enabled them to withstand the impacts of the global
economic downturn and associated falling copper price. According
to the managers, if Sino-Metals was just using its own resources of
copper tailings from the NFCA mine[24] in the MFEZ they 'should be
winding up now' but they could produce indefinitely, particularly as
they were now getting access to copper oxide from the Democratic
Republic of the Congo.

The controversial nature of labour relations at Chinese companies
was also noted by a trade union official, who argued that 'Most
Chinese do not pay overtime – just taken as normal working conditions, most workers are employed on short contracts and are not
provided with protective clothing'.[25] Further, the same union official
insisted that the Ministry of Labour rarely monitors the working conditions of employees in these companies, owing arguably to logistical
difficulties, and that labour laws needed to be amended to incor-
porate a 'minimum wage clause'.[26] However, overall, the union official
admitted that Chinese investment had wrought positive effects on
the Zambian economy, but that there was a need for regulation.
One employee of a Chinese company noted that 'labour laws are
being trampled on by the Chinese' and that inspectors from the
Ministry of Labour 'favour the Chinese not the local people'.[27] Eleven
Zambian miners were shot by Chinese managers at a coal mine
located approximately three hundred kilometres south of Lusaka
in 2010 for protesting against wage cuts (Laing 2010). After this the

Zambian home affairs minister 'urged the Chinese investors not to use firearms on innocent people' (Lusaka Times 2010). In 2012 a Chinese manager was killed and another seriously wounded at the Collum Coal mine, after the company reportedly did not raise wages in line with a government directive (Reuters 2012).

Weak labour regulation may be a way of attracting inward FDI, with an official at the United Nations Economic Commission for Africa (UNECA) arguing that Chinese investors could 'come here and do whatever they want'.[28] While some might see this as a governance failure,[29] another way to look at it is as a mode of governance; a particular kind of geo-governmentality involving a degree of self- (under-) regulation. The UNECA official noted that there was a power imbalance between African and the Chinese government but that lack of political conditionality attached to Chinese engagement 'goes down very well with [African] governments'.

It is sometimes noted that while China has an Africa strategy, Africa needs a China strategy (Alden 2005; Cheru and Calais 2010). However, this neglects the fact that African political elites already have a China strategy, which is to use it as a counterweight to Western conditionality and thereby bolster their own rule. There is thus an implicit 'liberal' bargain between them. African governments do not, for the most part, impose regulations on Chinese investment, while the Chinese government does not impose political conditions on African state elites. A sign over the headquarters of the CNMC in the MFEZ reads 'Zambia and China Cooperate for Common De- velopment'. It might more accurately read 'Zambian and Chinese political elites cooperate for mutual advantage', although the election of the new president, Michael Sata, in 2011, discussed below, who ran on a platform critical of China, has partially changed this, if not the underlying geopolitical opportunity structure. As a manager from the Zambia–China Mulungushi Textile Factory noted, echoing theories of dependency, 'instead of winning the confidence of the employees, the Chinese action was to win the politicians' confidence' (quoted in Brooks 2010: 130). This has led some to argue that 'in this way, China's interactions with the continent fit the pattern of most external actors' intercourse with Africa: beneficial to the ruling elite but to the long-term disadvantage of Africa's peoples' (Taylor

2010: 81). There have been employment benefits from the MFEZ in Zambia, however.

While there have been export processing and free trade zones in operation in different countries and territories such as Ireland and Puerto Rico for decades, the MFEZ is an example of a new hybrid type of globalization in action which potentially brings together both direct state capital and private resources, finances, markets and labour from different parts of the world. It is located in (relatively) politically stable Zambia, but able to access natural resources from the Democratic Republic of the Congo. More than 90 per cent of the DRC's resource-rich Katanga Province's exports are reportedly destined for China (Raine 2009). Consequently, Chinese geo-governance is arguably regional in nature.

'Reliable in politics, perfect in technique, and good at [a] tough fight': 'soft power' projects in Zambia

James Ferguson has noted that neoliberalism in Zambia occasioned a shift from 'thick' to socially 'thin' extractive industries (Ferguson 2006). In the initial post-independence period, the nationalized Zambia Consolidated Copper Mines (ZCCM) provided housing, education and healthcare for its employees. However, when the mines were privatized these obligations were shed, for the most part. Nonetheless, some limited healthcare facilities are still provided for mine employees, at least in the case of the Chinese NFCA mine in Chambishi (see Lungu and Mulenga 2005). According to the well-known political scientist Joseph Nye (2004), soft power refers to the ability to acculturate other states and societies to your values and consequently your interests. Some Chinese projects in Zambia may fall under this rubric, as discussed below.

The Sino-Zambian Friendship Hospital is located in Kitwe in Copperbelt Province. It was initially part of ZCCM, but is now a division of NFCA.[30] This hospital has forty-one beds and provides free healthcare, with mine managers' approval, for NFCA employees and one designated relative each. According to the chief medical officer, medical services were provided to NFCA employees as long as he was 'told by people there it was OK'. This is in addition to twenty-three companies from the local community which send their employees to the hospital on a paying basis.[31] The fact that healthcare is provided free only to NFCA workers and one relative shows a productionist, rather than a welfarist, orientation to the labour regime at NFCA. The company obviously wants a relatively healthy and productive labour force, but ownership of the hospital may also enable greater control of labour outside of the production process. When one of the workers at the Chinese-managed Mulungushi Textile factory in Kabwe was injured, 'the management at the company contrived with the hospital [in Kabwe] to destroy or hide the file ... Without this information it is very difficult ... for me to be compensated in the future ... maybe the company wanted to run away from its responsibility ...' (quoted in Brooks 2010: 125).

Nonetheless, it is significant that the NFCA feels that it needs to socially embed itself in the locality, as evidenced by the name of the hospital and the fact that it sponsors other social infrastructure, such as bus shelters in the region. As such it could be seen as a 'soft power' complement to 'harder power' economic projects such as the Chambishi Copper Smelter. Chinese and other current mining investment is, however, economically thin. While there were seventy so-called 'sprinter companies' – firms that supplied and supported the ZCCM mining conglomerate during the first post-independence copper boom – none of these is now in existence (Kragelund 2009b).

There are also other soft power projects which were implemented by China in Copperbelt Province, particularly the 'Friendship Stadium' in Ndola, which opened in 2012, and another in the capital, Lusaka. The Copperbelt and Lusaka are the two anchor regions for Chinese economic engagement in Zambia as they have received the most investment and migration from China, and consequently the choice of location for the stadia is perhaps not accidental. These are also the two regions which voted heavily for Michael Sata in the 2006 presidential elections, and the 2008 presidential by-elections, and they are also the two most economically important regions of the country.[32]

The stadium in Ndola has a capacity of 40,000 and covers an area of 203,300 square metres.[33] The construction company has built many Chinese embassies in Africa and works closely with the Chinese government, as evidenced by an extract from its website, which reads:

Foreign Aid Dept. [sic] of the Ministry of Commerce sent a letter of appreciation to AFECG for its initiative in foreign affairs and active contributions made to strengthening friendly relationship between China & Madagascar. The letter highly praised AFECG because it had greatly valued politics, overall situations and strictly followed the order of 'Immediate Commencement' given by the Ministry of Commerce in the course of implementation of Chinese-aided project of Madagascar International Conference Center when the condition for work commencement was not yet available. This embodied that AFECG, reliable in politics, perfect in technique, and good at tough fight, is an excellent foreign aid construction team. (AFECG 2010)

The Chinese government is known to finance and construct stadia and presidential palaces, such as the one for the president of Sudan, in Africa in order to build trust and rapport with populations and elites respectively. However, there are also some economic spin-offs from these construction projects, as they allow Chinese companies to enter new domestic and regional markets, many of the inputs are sourced in China and the AFECG is a provincial SOE, for example. The government of Zambia took out a loan from the Chinese government to build the Ndola stadium (Lusaka Times 2009).

At least fifteen Asian-owned construction companies in Zambia have won contracts ranging from maintenance to building of infrastructure, such as roads, railways and airports (National Council for Construction 2009). According to an official at the Ministry of Industry and Commerce in Zambia, 'the Chinese are now also dominating the construction sector'.[34] The Bank of China provides bid bond security, which guarantees that the difference in price compared to the next-lowest bid will be paid if a contractor fails to complete the work for Chinese construction companies in Zambia, putting them at a substantial competitive advantage (Kragelund 2009b). This is facilitated by the need to recycle China's huge foreign exchange reserves, which run into trillions of dollars.

In terms of inputs to build the stadium in Ndola, a civil engineer on the site noted 'everything is coming from China', demonstrating that even 'soft power' projects have economic pay-offs.[35] Another

Chinese construction company employee who was interviewed noted that the fact that there was 'no [industrial] infrastructure' in Zambia made things very difficult as they had to source cement from South Africa.[36] Although there are some cement production factories in Zambia, in the city of Ndola, for example, the building boom in the country meant there was local undersupply. Other Asian companies noted in a survey that the lack of industrial base provided them with a competitive advantage and that average low incomes (poverty) meant there was a market in Zambia for the cheap goods they produce (Carmody and Hampwaye 2010).

When the construction site of the stadium was visited in August 2009, the bricklayers were Chinese, while Zambians were confined to tasks such as mixing cement. The total number of workers at the time of the research was 220, out which 120 were Chinese.[37] This is despite the fact that under Zambian law there are meant to be a maximum of five expatriates working for any one company (US Commercial Service 2009). The other Chinese construction company whose representative was interviewed employed sixty Zambians and eight Chinese on their site. According to Moyo (2012), in Zambia Chinese companies hire, on average, fifteen locals for every Chinese expatriate, as compared to one to one in Angola but this has nonetheless been a politically contentious issue in the country.

Chinese entrepreneurial projects and the state

According to Kragelund (2009a) the average size of Chinese investments in Zambia fell from US$2 million in 2000 to approximately $1.4 million in 2006. This suggests the growing importance of private entrepreneurial, rather than large-scale state-owned, investment during that time, although it should also be noted that during the recent global economic recession, many small-scale Chinese-owned mines in Zambia closed, while some large state-owned conglomerates saw a buying opportunity (Herbst and Mills 2009; Carmody and Hampwaye 2010). However, as the discussion below shows, even some seemingly small-scale 'private' entrepreneurial migration and investment from China to Africa may be state linked.

The number of Chinese citizens resident in Zambia rose from 300 in 1992 to 80,000 currently. A number of owners of small-scale Chinese investments were also interviewed as part of this study. One of the things which was evident from the interviews was the 'snowball' or chain nature of Chinese engagement in Zambia. One Chinese doctor who was interviewed noted that she had come to Zambia first, but that her sister had followed her, along with her mother and father, and then another sister and brother.[38] Her brother operated a small-scale mine in Zambia, while her spouse and child remained in China. The goal was to work in the country for ten years and then return to China, where the spouse was a 'high' government official. In China, people who work in government while their spouses emigrate are known as *luo guan* (Beijing Review 2009).

In 2009, Shenzhen City banned *luo guan* from holding leadership positions in government in order to combat corruption after a study by Peking University found that more than ten thousand corrupt officials had fled overseas to join their families over the previous decade, taking US$96 billion in illegal income with them (ibid.). China punishes corruption heavily, including through the use of the death penalty, although there is no suggestion that our interviewee was in any way involved in corrupt practices.

Another small business owner who was interviewed was a travel agent specializing in the Chinese market. This entrepreneur immigrated to Zambia because of personal connections and also, as noted earlier, the presence of the Bank of China in the country.[39] They had recently also opened an office in Beijing. This interviewee noted that most new Chinese companies in Zambia were state owned and that there were not many 'personal people [entrepreneurs]'. Much of their business was consequently from state-owned companies. They noted that the global economic slowdown of 2008/09 had not affected their business, as the level of economic engagement between China and Zambia continued to deepen. While some current Chinese entrepreneurial investments have direct or indirect links to the Chinese state, this may change as they proliferate and become more embedded in Zambia.

Chinese structural power in Zambia

The structural power, or ability to set the rules of the game, of Chinese business and the state is also in evidence in relation to complaints about sub-standard goods, many of which are imported from China. According to officials at the Ministry of Industry and Commerce, the Zambian Bureau of Standards has both Voluntary and Compulsory Standards, and if imported products do not meet the latter they can be impounded or destroyed.[40] Zambian producers can also apply for safeguard measures against import surges, from China, for example, but none has done so to date as 'there are other consequences if you do not do it nicely or well' – another example of self- (under-) regulation or geo-governmentality.

The Chinese presence in Zambia is undergoing further deepening and embedding. As noted earlier with the global economic downturn, some Chinese companies took the opportunity to buy assets in Zambia from Western, Israeli and other investors, such as the Luanshya Copper Mine, at bargain basement prices. The mine was sold to the CNMC in 2009 for US$50 million (Lusaka Times 2009). Interestingly, the agreement was signed by the Chinese ambassador in Zambia, in addition to officials from the company. As a result of the global economic crisis, in contrast to earlier years, there was 'a lot of goodwill towards the Chinese in Copperbelt Province as they didn't run away' but kept investing.[41] This is facilitated by the fact that Chinese state-owned enterprises operate on thirty- to forty-year time horizons and that the Chinese government is eager to recycle its foreign exchange reserves overseas.

According to the country manager for the African Trade Insurance Agency, which shares risks of loan defaults by foreign investors with banks, 'some smart minds kept investing' as they knew the crisis would end.[42] Others argue that Chinese financial institutions are investing in Africa in a counter-cyclical manner (Davies 2009). This continuing investment in the face of the copper price declining by two-thirds is one reason why the 2008 presidential by-election was not marked by the same anti-Chinese sentiment as was in evidence in the 2006 election (see Negi 2008).

In Zambia, there have been allegations that the Chinese government is overly influential, with a Chinese deputy minister reportedly holidaying with the Zambian president and corruption allegations around government purchases of 100 hearses at inflated prices from China.[43] This influence is manifest in several other ways with other donors sometimes hearing about Chinese initiatives only through the media. According to a governance specialist at the Norwegian embassy, in relation to the MFEZ 'it was completely unannounced beforehand, nobody knew that Zambia was to have export processing zones where you had no taxes' (quoted in Haglund 2008: 556), although according to the former Zambian minister of commerce, trade and industry the MFEZ fell under the Triangle of Hope initiative sponsored by Japan (Mutati 2009).

Chinese business people are aware of the influence that the Chinese government has in Zambia. According to one, 'if you have a small problem you pay money. If you have a big problem report to the [Chinese] government.'[44] In a survey of firms from thirty countries, Transparency International found Chinese firms to be the most likely to pay bribes (Transparency International 2006, cited in Haglund 2008). Haglund also details evidence of tax evasion and transfer pricing by Chinese companies in Zambia.

The globalization of the Chinese state in Zambia

The evidence presented in this chapter would seem to support Tull's (2006: 469) argument that there is 'an interconnectedness of political, diplomatic and economic interests' in China's economic engagement in Africa. Under the Chinese government 'go out' policy, the Chinese Ministry of Commerce provides financial incentives, market intelligence and coordination for Chinese companies investing overseas (Haglund 2009). As a result Chinese investors in Africa put 'government support' as the second-most important reason for investing there (Broadman and Isik 2007).

According to the chairman of the Zambian Citizen Economic Empowerment Commission, 90 per cent of the Zambian population own only 10 per cent of the economy (Kragelund 2009c). This statistic is unlikely to change substantially as a result of the modes of geo-governance detailed in this chapter, as Chinese influence and economic power are embedded in Zambia. In 2008 Zambia collected only US$30 million in taxes on copper exports of US$2 billion (Collier 2010). If it had the same taxation regime as Chile it would have collected hundreds of millions in tax revenue. However, in contradiction of assumptions about China reinforcing authoritarianism in Africa,

Zambia's scores on political rights and civil liberties have shown general improvement since 2002 (Freedom House various), perhaps suggesting variegated impacts across regime types, although there does not appear to be a generalizable relationship (Solignac-Lecomte 2013).

While many Chinese actors are relatively autonomous of the Chinese state, they are often linked to it in multiple and complex ways. It is from these multiple hybridities, among these and other actors, that globalization's developmental outcomes are organized. This chapter has sought to qualify the dominant view to show how the model of Chinese globalization being pursued in Africa is fundamentally state driven, inspired and linked, if not coordinated. The Chinese state in Zambia exercises dethority and authority through mechanisms such as debt relief and contraction, and investment and market access, combined with threats to take these away, as happened before the 2006 presidential election, when the Chinese ambassador threatened to break diplomatic and economic relations if an anti-Chinese populist was elected. Ultimately Sata was elected in 2011, but only after he had substantially moderated his stance towards Chinese investment. Whereas previously he had said Zambia needed 'investors not infestors', by 2010 he was writing that 'Zambia needs international investors more than they need us' (quoted in Chellah 2010, in Fraser 2010: 21). After his election, his first official visitor was the Chinese ambassador.

While Sata's government has increased minimum wages, it also quickly reversed a ban on copper exports in less than a week, which was meant to allow time to better regulate the sector (Bariyo and Maylie 2011).[45] Thus the overall structure of geo-governance remains intact, which means 'the workforce [exploding] in violent protest on a relatively frequent basis but to little apparent long-term effect' (Fraser 2010: 3) is likely to continue.

A new regime of embedded geo-governance is being constructed in Zambia, and perhaps elsewhere in Africa, with distinctive characteristics based on an (il)liberal bargain between domestic and Chinese political elites. While there have been some benefits to Zambia in terms of employment creation and poverty reduction (Carmody 2010), a dependency on China is being created whereby the structural transformation of Zambia's economy is likely to remain blocked by the contours of this bargain of natural resources in exchange for support for regime maintenance through foreign investment and trade, barring further mass mobilization for a fairer sharing of the benefits of natural resources. As a result the power of the Chinese state to shape the governance regime in Zambia has deepened, as this chapter has demonstrated. Rather than globalization leading to the withering away of the state (Mbaye 2010), the Chinese state is directly involved in shaping economic globalization to its own advantage. Globalization requires an internationalization and respatialization of the power of the state to break down barriers to markets and directly access resources for companies, particularly in a context of increasing scarcity, as the Zambian case demonstrates. Zambia is being integrated into Chinese-centred global production networks, many of which are state owned. As such the power of the Chinese state is being respatialized and globalized, rather than simply reduced. While both China and Zambia are a part of South Space, huge power differentials exist between them, as this chapter has demonstrated. This power inequality allows the Chinese state to exercise substantial influence through a variety of channels, including at regional level. As the next chapter explores, Chinese geo-governance is also becoming intertwined with that of South Africa on the continent in particular.

3 | SOUTH AFRICA: ANOTHER BRIC IN THE WALL?[1]

South African interests in Africa

As the previous chapter explored, globalization is transforming the nature of authority in international relations, as hegemony is replaced by geo-governance, involving a more varied set of actors. However, private authority over markets and resources is still often constituted and refracted through states. Much has been written about China and India's rising role in sub-Saharan Africa, but South Africa remains a highly significant regional political and economic player. As noted earlier, facilitated through its regional leadership, it has also recently acceded to the BRIC cooperation mechanism, reflecting its growing international influence and the transforming nature of global governance. This chapter considers 'South African' geo-governance and its impacts in sub-Saharan Africa to explore the nature and construction of the power of the South African state, and its international influence. The 'power' of the South African state is increasingly intertwined with and infused with that of the Chinese state and transnational capital, as detailed below. The chapter concludes with reflections on how the South African case informs international relations and development theory.

There has recently been much media and academic interest in Chinese, and also Indian, investment in Africa (see Cheru and Obi 2010, for example); however, South Africa (SA) remains a very important regional influence as a result of the size of its economy, the power of its state and the nature of capital–state interactions. For example, in 2006 South African trade with the rest of Africa was about a third that of China's with the rest of Africa (Daniel and Bhengu 2009), despite it having a much smaller economy, and SA was the largest single foreign investor in the rest of the continent (Adebajo 2010). The power of South African corporations over the state is largely structural (e.g. to withhold economic investment) rather than instrumental, as they are largely 'white' owned and dominated, while state elites are largely 'black'. However, both groups share an interest in growing SA's economy, partly through regional expansion, to facilitate profit-making, development and regime maintenance. Furthermore, more than half of the ruling African National Congress (ANC) members of parliament were directors of companies in 2007, and President Zuma's wives and other relatives own around a hundred companies (Southern African Report 2011; *Mail and Guardian*, in Clark 2012).[2]

This chapter explores South African economic interests in sub-Saharan Africa (SSA) and how these articulate with distantiated power projection by the South African state – in both formal, through the New Partnership for African Development (NEPAD), and less formal bilateral relations – to influence development on the subcontinent and the construction of the South African state itself. SA has recently been able to leverage its growing regional influence to accede to the BRIC cooperation mechanism (People's Daily Online 2010). SA accommodates global and regional power interests on the continent, making it a 'gregional' state and power.

Given its relatively small economy, in global terms, South Africa has sought influence in Africa through its own geo-governance strategies. According to Thabo Mbeki, when he was deputy president of SA, 'we should not humiliate ourselves by pretending that we have strength which we do not have' (quoted in Barber 2004: 110, in Adebajo 2010: 150). This led to a different mode of operation whereby, through its trade and investment relations, South Africa serves as a site from which globalization is transmitted to the rest of SSA. Geo-governance is distinct from 'soft power' (Nye 2004) – an excessively state-focused concept relying on cultural affinity – as it also involves economic incentives.

South Africa functions as a 'gregional' or 'middleman' state for major powers and transnational capital, some of which originates in South Africa as it manipulates 'regional relations to navigate globalisation' (Hentz 2008: 490). In particular it seeks to promote economic liberalization to facilitate regional market access and governance by 'its' corporations. This is facilitated by regional political elites, but sometimes generates popular resistance, meaning that the South African state and other transnational forces with which it is imbricated succeed in achieving geo-governance regionally, but not Gramscian hegemony, which is informed by popular consent.

Dimensions of influence: what makes South Africa a major economic and political power on the continent?

South Africa is both an old and a new economic power on the subcontinent: old in that it has long had the biggest economy in SSA, and new because its companies and government have emerged from economic sanctions and capital controls as a result of the abolition of apartheid roughly twenty years ago. South Africa's economy accounts for about 80 per cent of the total for the Southern African Development Community (SADC), with thirteen member countries (Adebajo et al. 2007). With a population of around fifty million people, it accounts for over a third of SSA's economy and seventeen of the top twenty companies in Africa are South African (Africa Report 2011). Increasing South African influence on the continent is also evidenced by the election of a South African to lead the African Union in 2012 – Nkosazana Dlamini-Zuma – and its setting up of its own international cooperation agency – the South African Development Partnership Agency. Previously 75 per cent of South Africa's development cooperation funding was channelled through multilateral organizations (Chahoud 2008).

With the winding down of apartheid and the loosening of capital controls, South African companies began to invest extensively in SSA. Thus, rather than being externally imposed through World Bank/IMF programmes, this was an example of globalization from the inside out, as South African conglomerates expanded into the rest of the continent (see Carmody 2007).

South African investment in the countries of the SADC totalled almost a billion dollars a year between 1994 and 2004, and the country ranked as one of the top three sources of foreign direct investment in ten of those countries (UNCTAD 2005, cited in Schroeder 2008). Among developing and transition economies South Africa is now the third-largest sender of FDI to the least developed countries, after India and China (UNCTAD 2012). Eighty per cent of South African investment in least developed countries was directed to two projects in Mozambique in 2011.

One of these investments was by the South African energy company Sasol. Its natural gas project in Mozambique recorded an investment of over US$1.8 billion in 2011, but somewhat shockingly created only an estimated 161 jobs directly (ibid.). Consequently this is an extremely capital-intensive investment, with each job 'costing' US$12 million. However, this project is deeply embedded in the political economy of the region, as both the Mozambican and the South African governments are partners in it (World Economic Forum on Africa 2010).

SA has actively encouraged regional expansion by its companies through the state-owned Industrial Development Corporation, which has invested in sixty projects in twenty-one countries. The SA Department of Trade and Industry also operates a 'Capital Projects Feasibility Programme', which 'is a cost-sharing scheme, providing a contribution to the cost of feasibility studies that are likely to lead to projects outside South Africa that will increase local exports and stimulate the market for the South African capital goods and services' (DTI 2010), with a higher rate of subsidy for African projects. The South African state also facilitates corporate penetration of the subcontinent through infrastructure development and bilateral ties, even with 'rogue' regimes, such as Zimbabwe.

In Tanzania almost 60 per cent of new foreign investment deals during 1996–98 were from South Africa (Söderbaum 2004). There are over 150 South African companies active there, although many locals boycott them, as they are 'white' and associated with colonialism. One Tanzanian pastoralist activist noted, 'we now live in the United States of South Africa' (quoted in Schroeder 2008: 24). This perception is a result of the penetration of South African *national capital*, defined by Schroeder (2012: 5) as 'a set of economic actors – investors, traders, industrialists – whose actions serve both individual and national intentions, whose national origins are clearly marked, and whose goods and services carry related associations and meanings abroad'. By 2005 only eight of the biggest 100 companies quoted on the Johannesburg Stock Exchange (JSE) did not have operations in Africa (Hudson 2007).

The regional expansion of SA companies was meant to be a component of the strategy to drive an economic renaissance there, and then in the region more generally. The main areas of SA outward investment into Africa were infrastructure (27 per cent in 2000–03), mining (22 per cent) and oil, gas and petroleum (18 per cent) (Daniel and Lutchman 2006, cited in Southall and Comninos 2009). By 2002 major SA companies such as AngloGold Ashanti and Mobile Telecommunications Networks (MTN) were deriving more than half of their profits from their African activities (UNCTAD 2005).

There are a variety of axes of South African engagement in Africa, including manufacturing and mining investment, but also services. The growth of South African corporates has, however, facilitated the more than 60 per cent expansion of the South African economy, in constant prices, from 1994 to 2009 (calculated from IMF 2011), facilitating SA's growing international influence and rise in the Index of Government Economic Power from 12th to 9th in the world from 2000 to 2009 (Basu et al. 2011). While SA is rhetorically committed to neoliberal 'good governance', economic interests take priority in its relations with SSA (Taylor 2011).

Channels of South African impact on sub-Saharan Africa

SA influences the economies of SSA through flows of trade, FDI and foreign portfolio investment (FPI). There are also influences from labour migration and remittances and the construction and exportation of governance regimes. Table 3.1 is illustrative (the categories and typology of relations are indicative and not mutually exclusive).

Common ways of describing trade are in terms of balance and terms of trade and the technological intensity of imports and exports. In SA's trade with SSA it is useful to assess whether trade is complementary, competitive, consumptive or extractive. Complementary trade is where both the sending and the receiving countries benefit. So, for example, if South Africa exports mining equipment, this facilitates economic growth in other countries, which more than compensates for the loss of capital associated with having to buy the mining equipment. Competitive trade is where there is direct competition between goods produced domestically and those coming from SA. If South African companies are more competitive than those in the region this leads to a double loss for SSA economies as companies are displaced, jobs and taxes are lost and the potential for learning-by-doing and multipliers and spillovers are forgone.

TABLE 3.1 South Africa's developmental impacts in sub-Saharan Africa

		Nature of relations with region			
	Trade	Outward foreign direct investment	Foreign portfolio investment	Labour and personal capital flows	Governance regimes and ideas
Capital extractive (results in net flow of capital to SA or overseas).	Consumptive (e.g. cars from SA) and competitive (e.g. textiles from SA).	Market serving (e.g. retail, bank and cell phone investment from SA).	Capital flows from region into SA stock market and banks.	Regional brain drain of skilled workers and professionals and economic/trade tourism to SA.	EU–SA free trade agreement (SA as regional entrepôt for EU goods).
Resource extractive (flow of resources to SA for further processing).	Extractive (e.g. copper to SA).	Export platform (e.g. minerals to SA).	Global FPI transformed in SA to outward FDI, often in resource sector.	Associated migration of South African 'expats' and local resentment.	Private sector driven – idea of South African-centred regional space economy.
Developmental (contributing to economic growth and/or poverty reduction).	Complementary (e.g. mining equipment from SA).	Various.	Capital flows from SA into regional stock markets and banks.	Return migration to countries of origin (brain circulation) and remittances.	NEPAD (infrastructural and educational development and peer review mechanism). Africa as a region of 'good governance'.

Type of impact

Consumptive trade is where goods are imported for non-productive purposes from South Africa, such as Mercedes to Zimbabwe, which remained one of the largest consumers of these in Africa despite its economic crisis (Lockwood 2005). In this case South Africa receives the benefits of the jobs created by assembly, although the profits flow (mostly) offshore to stockholders.

Extractive trade is where minerals are mined for processing by South African companies and the profits remitted to South Africa. Given the prominence of South African conglomerates in these areas this is a common pattern in SSA. Since the end of apartheid, SA has had a highly favourable trade balance with SSA; often of the order of eight to one, although this has narrowed more recently. Trade then forms an important aspect of the South African-led geo-governance matrix shown above.

The Lucas paradox, whereby richer countries, rather than exporting capital, as predicted by conventional theory, actually receive net capital also appears to operate in SA's relations with the region. For example, total South African investment in Botswana, Lesotho, Swaziland, Namibia, Zimbabwe and Mauritius is 4 per cent less than those countries' investments in South Africa (calculated from South African Reserve Bank 2010).

In SA's case, however, capital also flows outwards, particularly as major South African conglomerates have listings on the London, New York and Dubai stock exchanges to denominate assets in hard currencies and get into stock market indices, which lower loan capital costs (Carmody 2007). South Africa is a net recipient of FPI (Hausmann and Andrews 2009), but is subject to dramatic outflows during times of economic turbulence, forcing high interest rates and reducing domestic economic growth (Bond and Zapiro 2006). In terms of the exact mechanisms, according to UNCTAD (2009a: 69–70):

> it would ... appear that portfolio investment into South Africa is financing FDI outflows from South Africa to the rest of the region. In effect, South Africa is trading financial assets for real assets in favour of the rest of the region thus using its relatively sophisticated financial markets to attract financial resources that are in turn invested across Africa.

South Africa, then, acts as a centre of capital conversion from FPI to FDI, with 95 per cent of FPI into the continent flowing into the JSE (Davies, cited in South African Government News Service 2011). South African companies have substantial regional impacts through their investments, as detailed below.

South African touristic and agricultural investment

As noted earlier, there are a variety of axes of South African economic engagement in Africa. Tourism is now thought to be the world's largest service sector industry. While Africa has traditionally had a low share of the global total (Rogerson 2007), it has experienced growth in recent years. South African companies are heavily involved in the tourism industry in the rest of Africa. Already by the early years of the new millennium Protea Hotels had resorts in nine African countries, whereas the comparable figure for Southern Sun was six (Daniel et al. 2003). Imperial car rental had 110 locations in eight southern African countries.

South African investment in tourism has substantial impacts in particular localities, both positive and negative. For example, according to Rogerson (2005: 117):

> in 2001 the tourism economy of Livingstone [Zambia] was transformed by the opening of two new hotels, the Zambezi Sun and the Royal Livingstone which are operated by the South African-based tourism multinational, Sun International. These two new resorts represented an investment of US$65 million and immediately increased direct tourism employment in Livingstone by a factor of 25%.

Furthermore, there was indirect employment creation and programmes to increase sourcing of food locally, one of which was supported by the World Bank. It is more powerful (often white) actors in global commodity chains, however, who capture most of the benefits (Lapeyre 2011). Livingstone has benefited from the 'Zimbabwe effect', as that country's travails mean that tourists prefer to see Victoria Falls from the Zambian side.

However, tourism may also involve displacement. The South African eco-safari group manages the 136,000-hectare Grumeti game reserve in Tanzania – which is roughly the size of the English county of Surrey – where a room costs US$1,875 a night (Pearce 2012). There locals have been excluded from bringing their cattle on to their traditional grazing lands.

There is a history of 'fortress conservation' originating from South Africa, with 17 per cent of the country devoted to private wildlife reserves (Snijders, quoted in ibid.: 275), and the World Wildlife Fund, which was founded by South African billionaire Anton Ruppert, previously paid for helicopter gunships to shoot poachers in Kenya (Pearce 2012). Ruppert was also involved in setting up the Peace Parks Foundation, which seeks to establish trans-frontier conservation areas across Africa. Relatedly the South African government has established a fund of almost half a billion US dollars to assist ('white') South African farmers outside of the country, as nearly a third of the country's farmland is set to be transferred to black owners by 2014.

'Land grabbing' has also been in evidence in the agricultural sector. For example, in Mozambique an agreement was signed with the South African government to allow its farmers to lease old Portuguese cotton farms of up to 200,000 hectares. Reportedly the South African high commissioner in Maputo said that 'tame Kafirs' from South Africa could manage local labourers on behalf of absentee landlords. In 1999, three years after the agreement was signed, only thirteen South African farmers had moved, and now there are only five, but the Mozambican government has offered another million hectares to them (ibid.).

In Zambia the South African sugar company Illovo[3] provides 10 per cent of all formal sector jobs, mostly in sugar cutting. In Mali the company had plans to develop a 14,000-hectare sugar plantation which would displace 1,600 people and could take an estimated billion cubic metres of water a year from the Niger river; potentially dramatically affecting downstream users.

'The Great Trek North': South African media and information and communication technology companies

In the nineteenth century Afrikaners undertook a 'Great Trek' east and north-east from the Western Cape in what is now South Africa to escape British rule. The recent migration of South African farmers to Nigeria and Mozambique has sometimes been presented as being reminiscent of this. However, others have spoken of a 'Great Trek' by South African media and information and communication technology companies into the rest of Africa (Tleane 2006).

In terms of print media this includes companies such as the *Mail and Guardian* and *Business Day*. There are also satellite television companies such as M-Net (previously Electronic Media Network) and radio services such as Channel Africa and internet service providers such as M-Web and Vox Telecom. Both M-Net and M-Web are owned by the South African media conglomerate Naspers. The expansion of South African media is not politically neutral as they inculcate consumerist norms, often to the benefit of other South African corporations. According to the Media Development and Diversity Agency (2009, quoted in Duncan 2011: 346), 'in post 1994 South Africa, the print media is still majority owned and controlled by white shareholders' and management are under increasing pressure to respond to commercial imperatives. Media, then, is an important component of geo-governmentality, and one of the competitive advantages that South African media bring to the region is that, in often restrictive media environments, the fact that they are foreign owned means they are less involved in domestic politics (Tleane 2006). Increasingly, however, young people are also receiving their media content over their mobile phones.

Africa has the highest proportion of mobile telephone users of total telephone users in the world (International Telecommunications Union 2007, cited in Sanchez 2008), with more than ten mobile phones for every landline (ITU 2009). So-called 'smart phone' use is now growing rapidly as these are sometimes available for less than US$100. There are a number of major South African mobile phone service providers active on the continent, particularly MTN (Mobile Telecommunications Network) and Vodacom, which is part owned by the British company Vodafone. According to Daniel (2006: 207): 'If there were an award for the best performing post-apartheid South African corporate in Africa, it would be won by MTN for what this company has achieved in Africa and beyond in less than a decade is remarkable.'

MTN is now the largest mobile telephone operator in Africa, with

TABLE 3.2 Knowledge economy indicators: South Africa compared to Organisation for Economic Co-operation and Development (OECD) countries

Percentage of gross domestic product spent on research and development (2006)	South Africa: 0.95	OECD average: 2.26
Number of researchers per thousand employed (2005)	South Africa: 1.4	OECD average: 7.3
Triadic patents per million population (2006)	South Africa: 0.6	Switzerland: 114.8
Exports of information and communication technology equipment (millions of US dollars, 2007)	South Africa: 1,142	Ireland: 23,532
ISO 9001 certifications (2008)	South Africa: 3,792	United Kingdom: 41,150

Sources: OECD (2009) and ISO (2009). Triadic patents refers to the number of patents registered in the European Union, Japan and the United States. International Standards Organization 9001 certifications are given for quality management systems.

a subscriber base of over 170 million in 2011, and operations in twenty-one countries in Africa and the Middle East (Southall and Comninos 2009; mobileworld 2012) employing over six thousand people (Monama 2009). MTN is a product of the government of South Africa's Black Economic Empowerment (BEE) initiative, and the fact that mobile telephony is a new economic activity meant that there was a niche for emergent 'black' business in this area.

Nigeria has become MTN's most profitable market. It was awarded a Global Systems Mobile licence there in 2001, and by 2003 had invested more than a billion US dollars in the country; by 2004 the company's profits in Nigeria surpassed those in South Africa (Daniel 2006). Over a quarter of MTN subscribers are now in Nigeria, as against only 13.3 per cent in South Africa (mobileworld 2012). According to Stiglitz (2010), foreign mobile telephone companies are 'mining' SSA countries of their wealth. For example, in Tanzania the poorest 75 per cent of the population who use mobile phones spend an average of 22 per cent of their monthly incomes on them (Gillwald and Stork 2008). In part this represents a flow of income from poor people to overseas stockholders in Vodacom, headquartered in South Africa, which is a major operator in that country.

Mobile telephony is one of the few areas where indigenous capitalist participation has been significant in Africa (Southall and Comninos 2009). This results from a confluence of factors, particularly the exploitation of market opportunity by a number of indigenous entrepreneurs, backed by state, multinational and private capital; the generally poor state of fixed line communications, which allowed the rapid penetration of mobile phones; liberalization and privatization of the telephony market; and finally rapid advances in technology. However, rather than propelling SSA into cutting-edge global production networks and thereby transforming production structures, mobile telephony, mineral extraction, retailing and banking might better be conceived of as creating thin forms of integration or 'thintegration' (Carmody 2010); making Africa an information society but not a knowledge economy, as the statistics on SA, Africa's most innovative economy, show (see Table 3.2). These figures indicate the extent of the development gap between SA and the rich world, and consequently SA has to exercise influence through other mechanisms.

Markets, minerals and migrants: South Africa's regional economic impacts

South African companies have rapidly expanded their presence throughout Africa in other areas. SSA was an attractive investment ground for South African companies because they were generally too small to compete in the developed world (Hudson 2007). While South African manufactures were not, for the most part, globally competitive after the end of apartheid, given sanctions and the particular economic incentive structures that prevailed prior to economic liberalization, they were competitive in the region, where they account for about 70 per cent of South African exports (competitive, consumptive and complementary trade). Indeed, South Africa has enjoyed trade surpluses with its neighbours, with a ratio of exports to imports of six to one in its favour in the late 1990s (Landsberg and Kornegay 1999, cited in Landsberg 2002). However, imports, largely raw materials (extractive trade), from the rest of Africa increased more than ninefold from 2000 to 2008,[4] and by 2009 this ratio was only two to one in South Africa's favour (calculated from Statistics South Africa 2010). In part this may be a result of re-exports to Asia, as copper from the Chinese special economic zone in Zambia is trans-shipped through Durban, for example.[5]

In 2002, the South African Department of Foreign Affairs argued that 'the current most important issues with regard to the Central African Region are conflict resolution, promotion of peace and stability and good governance and reconstruction and development' (quoted in Landsberg 2002: 169). The other main priority, it argued, was the expansion of economic relations with the region. According to the head of the local economic development unit of eThekwini municipality in South Africa, 'our own market doesn't have the numbers to put us in a competitive position' in manufacturing, and South Africa can't compete with low-cost producers internationally.[6] Consequently the focus is on developing manufacturing for the regional market – the 'sub-Sahara'. According to this informant, NEPAD's infrastructural projects, such as road and rail, will allow more access to SSA. South Africa has floated bonds to raise money for infrastructure development in the region (Moyo 2009).

With echoes of colonialism, it was also felt that political stability promoted by NEPAD would facilitate commerce. However, the existing types of economic engagement in the Great Lakes region, for example, may have facilitated or fomented conflict. A United Nations report to the General Assembly cited twelve South African companies which may have been involved in the looting of minerals during the war in the Democratic Republic of the Congo (Hudson 2007).

The massively increased presence of South African companies and trade in SSA has been highly contentious in other countries. For example, some Zimbabwean business people accused SA of deliberately trying to deindustrialize the country (Landsberg 2002). A loan from the SA government to Zimbabwe for half a billion dollars reportedly contained conditionalities promoting economic liberalization (Bond 2006a).

Many formal retailers in Africa also find themselves under increasing pressure from South African supermarkets in particular. For example, the major South African retailer, Shoprite, with operations across Africa and also now in India, by the early 2000s reportedly contributed 2 billion rand, or around US$400 million, to South Africa's exports (Naidu and Lutchman 2005, cited in Miller et al. 2008). Also, Tiger Brands, which is South Africa's largest food company, has recently invested heavily in Nigeria, taking a 63.5 per cent stake in Dangote Flour Mills for US$183 million, among other investments (Alinyeju 2012).

Shoprite is planning seventy new stores in Nigeria, and these chains serve as important engines of intra-African trade, but often import much of their produce from SA (Rundell 2010). This, along with the scale of other SA investment, has given rise to fears of neocolonialism in the region. Speaking of South African investment in Africa, the managing director of a Shoprite subsidiary spoke of 'an army on the move' (Barber 2004: 179, quoted in Adebajo 2010: 113).

In a little over ten years after the fall of apartheid, South African companies acquired controlling stakes in Tanzania's national brewery, airline and largest banking chain (Schroeder 2008). In Kenya there was a so-called 'beer war' between SABMiller (South African Breweries-Miller) and Kenya's national brewery, which ended when the two agreed to grant each other effective near-monopolies in Tanzania and Kenya respectively. According to one executive, 'SABMiller went away with their tail between their legs [in Kenya]. There was real consumer resistance to the South African product' (quoted in Rundell 2010: 44). In response to issues such as these SABMiller now makes an effort to source inputs locally, and in the new country of South Sudan it reportedly wants to help 2,000 smallholders grow cassava for its beer (Pearce 2012). However, the agreement by SABMiller (2013) to distribute its rival's beer in Kenya ended in 2010, and some see a new 'beer war' in the offing (Wahome 2012).

Shoprite also had a policy of embedding through sourcing fresh produce locally in the African countries in which it operates. In Zambia one Asian company, which had undergone a major investment expansion to supply Shoprite, noted that its contract had been cancelled as the corporation was favouring SA producers instead (Carmody and Hampwaye 2010), perhaps influenced by SA's 'Proudly South African' campaign. This national/regional tension is evidenced in the title of the group's 2005 annual report, *Proudly South Africa, Proudly African*, in which it is emphasized that the company is 'growing with Africa' (Shoprite 2005).

The return on average capital employed was an incredible 50 per cent for the company during 2004/05. As most of the stock market remains in 'white' hands (England 2011), statistics such as these are one of the reasons why post-apartheid inequality in SA increased, as did extreme poverty (Hoogveen and Ozler 2005), although a wider social safety net has recently changed this (Marais 2010). Rising inequality and deepening poverty for some of SA's population make it attractive for some corporates to focus on regional investments more to serve the middle classes in neighbouring countries than the impoverished masses at home, where urban poverty appears to be increasing (Maharaj et al. 2010).

As noted in Shoprite's (2003: 2) annual report, 'the Group's objective for growth outside South Africa is to gain a foothold in the most lucrative markets as soon as possible'. The number of Shoprite stores in Africa, outside of South Africa, increased by over 30 per cent from 2003 to 2010. While this may have contributed to formal sector employment growth in the receiving countries, the vast majority of Shoprite's workers in Zambia, for example, are casual, with some likening their wages to conditions of slavery (Miller 2005).

Other South African investments have been highly controversial because they have resulted in forced displacement. In 1997 hundreds of small-scale gemstone miners were forcibly removed from the 12-square-kilometre area of Tanzania where the precious stone tanzanite is found. The South African company which now mines it, TazaniteOne, aims to make it a gift associated with births and markets its products to high-income consumers in South Africa and abroad. Thus the same commodity can have very different meanings – joy over family expansion, or displacement and loss of livelihood (Schroeder 2010).

In addition to these channels South Africa has also attracted highly skilled workers from SSA, but also loses highly skilled personnel to rich countries. In 2001, 18 per cent of the outflow of research and development staff in South Africa's scientific councils was to jobs overseas (Kahn 2004). There is, however, a certain amount of 'brain circulation' as knowledge workers leave and come back, and South Africa attracts them from the region. However, the impact of South Africa on the region is one of brain drain, as the country arguably attempts to move up the surplus value chain.

At the same time as South Africa has attracted highly skilled immigrants, it has shut out low-skilled ones. This had dramatic impacts in Lesotho as the proportion of gross national product accounted for by remittances fell from 62 per cent to 18 per cent in the decade after 1990 (Hassan 2002). The vast majority of remittances in Lesotho are used for household subsistence, rather than savings or investment (Crush et al. 2010). As SA does not keep detailed records, data on the scale of remittance outflows from the country are not available (Gupta et al. 2007). The fact that there is a major transnational migrant labour system in southern Africa, of which South Africa is the hub, has also dramatically increased the prevalence of HIV in the region as a result of family separation and disruption (Campbell 2003).

In sum, this section has explored South African economic engagement across a number of sectors. The primacy of profit in South African corporate engagement is evident, as is the competitive displacement of local businesses, and sometimes people, by more powerful South African business actors. However, the impacts of South African corporate engagement have been contradictory, as they have also often increased investment and formal sector jobs. This contradictory economic configuration requires an attendant mode of regulatory governance, which the next section discusses.

The rise of the south in Africa: 'South African' geo-goverance in sub-Saharan Africa

Some have argued that South Africa performs a 'sub-imperial' role in Africa (Bond and Zapiro 2006), as a gateway for Western interests, or that it is attempting to be a regional hegemon in its own right. However, particularly given its own economic problems, it has found regional hegemonic status difficult to achieve, although under Nelson Mandela it did intervene militarily in Lesotho. But South Africa is both a 'region-organizing' state, through its leadership role in organizations such as SADC, and a 'region-mobilizing' state, through its cultivation of economic and strategic ties with neighbouring states (Vom Hau et al. 2012). It has pursued a strategy whereby 'emergence of a regional presence [is] the *sine qua non* for being taken seriously globally' (Mistry 1999: 133, quoted in Hentz 2008: 493). The South African state consequently uses the region as a springboard to the global, in part by facilitating global forces' access to the region. SA's global presence, then, in turn, increases its regional influence.

During the late 1990s and early 2000s much was written about the developmental potential of the 'new regionalism' whereby neighbouring countries in the global South could establish new institutions of coordination in contradistinction to those of neoliberalism. However, in practice so-called 'open regionalism', which favoured global integration, took precedence. Prior to the end of apartheid only around 8 per cent of South Africa's trade was with the rest of the continent, but this has now risen to almost 11 per cent (calculated from Statistics South Africa 2011). Has the reintegration of South Africa's economy resulted in the creation of a new regional economic space?

Rather than being natural artefacts, regions are geographical areas defined by sets of social and economic practices. '"Regionalization" refers to the process of cooperation, integration, cohesion and identity creating a regional space' (Söderbaum 2004: 7), and this is 'preceded by the existence of region builders' (Neumann 2003: 161).

When the ANC-led government came to power in 1994 it had to balance the demands and expectations of those who were disenfranchised and immiserized by apartheid with the structural power of those who had been enriched by the previous system (Hentz 2005). One way to attempt to achieve this was through regional market opening, which it was hoped would create both jobs and profits for South African companies. However, in order for market opening to be achieved there had to be consent on the part of other African states and a move away from the use of force.

According to Grieco and Ikenberry (2003: 112, quoted in Schoeman 2007: 104), a hegemon must 'use its domestic market to stabilise the larger continental economy and it must be able to resist domestic pressures to look out only for its citizens' own interests'. Given the challenges facing the South African economy itself, Thabo Mbeki, the former president of South Africa, attempted to find a way out of this conundrum: the need for acceptance of South African leadership in the region, to allow its companies to expand in Africa, without the economic resources to back it up through the idea of African Renaissance and in particular NEPAD, promoted by South Africa. Adebajo (2008) calls this 'hegemony on a shoestring'.

NEPAD (2001) was, in essence, meant to be a bargain between the rich countries and Africa, whereby African governments would agree to the peer review of their governance by an eminent persons group, in order to improve their performance, in exchange for more trade, aid and investment from the West. However, some question the link between NEPAD and SA investment in SSA, which they argue is largely ad hoc and takes place outside of government-inspired frameworks (Alden and Le Pere 2009).

Former president Wade of Senegal, who was involved in designing NEPAD, has criticized it as highly ineffectual. According to him, 'expenses adding up to hundreds of millions of dollars have been spent on trips, on hotels. But not a single classroom has been built, not a single health centre completed. NEPAD has not done what it was set up for' (quoted in Djité 2008: 195). An economist involved in designing the programme noted that it was 'dead'. However, President Zuma (2010a) has argued that NEPAD, through infrastructure development, can transform the economies of the continent and overcome the effects of colonialism. While little has been done to date, discourse is important in generating consent for corporate penetration, and Zuma says: 'we will support efforts to speed up the political and economic integration of the SADC region, and promote intra-regional trade and investment', and 'intensify efforts to promote the interests of South Africa globally' (quoted in Zuma 2010b).

NEPAD fits with ideas of 'good' or matrix governance, which seeks to establish and coordinate networks of actors; to regularize the chaotic flows and relations of globalization – to establish a mode of regulation for the neoliberal regime of accumulation in the (under)developing world, and achieve access to resources (Carmody

2010). Through deregulation and the protection of private property the state is to foster the conditions for market governance and, in theory, for the private sector to flourish (Harrison 2005): a 'matrix state' (Martinez 1999). NEPAD, then, in addition to its infrastructural dimensions, is an attempt to produce a regionalized space of 'good' governance – to facilitate capital accumulation, economic develop-ment and the fulfilment of human rights – but this is an ambitious task given the diversity of African state-society formations and the inherent contradictions of the project.

When SA was the only African government to condemn the human rights abuses of Sani Abacha, the Nigerian military dictator in the 1990s, it showed itself to be out of step with most other African leaderships, who value regime survival above everything else, given the economic benefits which flow from it (Clark 2002). This partly explains why Mandela's successor, Thabo Mbeki, adopted a 'softly, softly' approach towards Robert Mugabe, and other African autocrats, which has been continued by his successor Jacob Zuma. According to the South African foreign minister such an approach was justi-fied because Africans don't like being talked down to as it reminds them of their colonial past (Adebajo 2010). Although a South African diplomat noted that Jacob Zuma has been very clear that 'South Africa should lead the region'. What South Africa has achieved is market access in exchange for political quiescence: corporate geo-governance (access to resources and markets for its companies), rather than hegemony.

The economic impacts of South Africa on the region have been contradictory. It has promoted investment, and hence job creation, but South African firms have out-competed domestic companies. At the same time rapid economic growth in South Africa, prior to the global economic downturn, meant there was a major and growing export market for the region. These dynamics articulate with other processes operating at different scales, such as the new inter-regionalism being forged with Asia and debt relief to create a new scalar alignment potentially favourable to African poverty reduction (Carmody 2010). However, the terms of South Africa's regional reintegration have been largely in its, as opposed to the region's, favour.

Future trends: the merger of South African and Chinese geo-governance?

There is an emerging middle and upper class in South Africa, but also a growing class gulf which impacts on governance and the region. According to Mzi Khumalo, chairman of Johannesburg Consolidated Investments, 'we are here to run a business. I am not for any of this brotherhood stuff' (quoted in Andreasson 2010: 275). Income inequality has worsened in post-apartheid SA as those with access to capital and skills have, in general, benefited from the more liberal economic regime.

While South Africa's economy was growing at 5–6 per cent before the global economic crisis, and jobs were being created for the first time in decades, increasing inequality and the unfulfilled promises of liberation were some of the most important factors in the rise of Jacob Zuma and the demise of Thabo Mbeki. However, Zuma may not sufficiently reflect the level of anger in the general population, which is perhaps best captured by the former leader of the ANC youth league, Julius Malema, whose rhetoric is similar to that of Robert Mugabe (Mbeki and Rossouw 2010). Some argue that this may be a 'Nongqawuse syndrome' (Andreasson 2010), Nongqawuse being a Xhosa millenarian prophet in the nineteenth century who encouraged people to slaughter their cattle. The Marikana mine massacres in 2012, when police killed thirty-four striking miners, set off a wave of other strikes, protests and repression across the country, with President Zuma forced to declare that the country was not at a 'tipping point' (SAPA 2012). This conjuncture reflects the contradiction between the particular (post-)apartheid model of accumulation and state legitimation. SA is attempting to strike a balance between its domestic economic and socio-political needs, through market opening in Africa, for example, and the broader interests of the region in order to legitimize such economic penetration, through international initiatives such as NEPAD, and taking a leading role in multilateral negotiations and institutions on 'Africa's' behalf. As such, South Africa is a 'gregional' state which attempts to balance global and regional interests to 'national' ends.

South Africa is, however, under pressure from the increasing Asian presence in Africa. For example, exports to Africa as a proportion of total exports were stagnant from 1998 at around 13–14 per cent (Martin 2008). Furthermore, exports to SADC countries actually declined to about a tenth of South Africa's total exports, suggesting that the relatively industrialized South African economy faces competitive pressures from Asia unlike those of many other African economies dominated by raw materials and primary production (ibid.). In relation to South Africa's trade relationship with China, the country largely exports minerals and receives manufactured goods such as machinery, textiles, footwear and clothing in return (Willcox and Van Seventer 2005). In fact, by the middle of last decade South Africa was exporting fewer advanced manufactured goods to China than it did in the early 1990s, while China, on the other hand, exported greater quantities of these to South Africa (ibid.).

Political power largely flows from economic power, and as the relative role of South Africa decreases, as compared to China's, its direct influence on the continent is likely to be more limited in the future, even as its indirect influence is transformed and more deeply interwoven with global social forces. According to Davies, 'what is naturally South Africa's regional commercial space is fast becoming China's' (quoted in Lee 2006: 322). In recognition of this the South African state is attempting to more deeply imbricate itself with, and leverage the power of, the Chinese state – signing a 'comprehensive strategic partnership' with it in 2010. Previously a Binational Commission had been established to analyse and review the relationship, and the trust which is accorded to South Africa in China is evidenced by the fact that Naspers is the biggest foreign media organization in the country (Centre for Chinese Studies 2007).

The Chinese strategy of flexigemony in Africa is also reflected in South African institutions, illustrated by the 20 per cent sale of the Standard Bank of South Africa, with its extensive branch network across Africa, to the Industrial and Commercial Bank of China for $5.5 billion in 2007, which boosted FDI in South Africa that year by hundreds of percentage points. According to Adebajo (2010: 197), 'this represented the largest foreign direct investment in South Africa's history, and could establish a future partnership for the economic domination of the continent, though both rivalry and cooperation are the more likely outcome of this growing bilateral relationship'.

SA accounts for 40 per cent of the total stock of Chinese FDI in Africa (UNCTAD 2010), and it is now a gateway for Chinese influence on the continent. Unlike with other countries, China voluntarily restrained exports of textile and clothing to SA in order to maintain good relations.

The growing influence of the BRICS powers in Africa is not a zero-sum game. For example, the banking group FirstRand has announced that it will refocus on Africa and take advantage of the growing regional links with China and India (Rundell 2010). The question is whether South Africa's own internal governance issues, structured by its mode of incorporation into the global political economy, mean it becomes part of a submerging, rather than an emerging, 'middle' of rising powers. (Car exports to the European Union fell 47.4 per cent from 2008 to 2009 as a result of the global financial crisis and stark inequality challenges internal governance, as evidenced by riots prior to the World Cup in SA, for example, and continuing unrest in the mining sector.) If this is the case, this will in turn compromise its ability to influence global governance regimes. However, if the contradictions of South Africa's develop- ment (in Africa) can continue to be contained, the current trajectory of increasing international influence is likely to be maintained. Writing of South Africa's accession to the BRICS, He Wenping (2011) argues that 'the strong economic links China has with South Africa ... can not only boost expansion of Sino-African relations overall but also set an example for, as well as guide and lead, the establish- ment of a new type of strategic partnership between China and Africa as a whole'.

The future of South African geo-governance

South Africa is one of the world's most unequal societies. This is a consequence of the political economy of apartheid and the particular path of economic liberalization pursued by the majority govern- ments. Some argue that South Africa is characterized by a 'double temporality' whereby the democratic state coexists with the reality of continued white domination of the economy (Barnard and Farred 2004). Current developments represent a modified reinscription of South African influence over if not domination of the subcontinent, in concert with other powers and transnational capital – corporate-led geo-governance.

The South African state has attempted to navigate the currents of globalization, by opening its economy and promoting market opening in Africa, while attempting to reform the system of global governance to be more favourable towards developing countries (Bond 2004). South Africa, then, serves as a conduit for globalized and marketized geo-governance in SSA. According to the ANC's director of policy: 'We don't oppose the WTO. We'd never join a call to abolish it, or to abolish the World Bank or the IMF. Should we be out there condemning imperialism? If you do those things, how long will you last? There is no organizational alternative, no real policy alternative to what we are doing' (quoted in Bond 2004, in Maharaj et al. 2010: 17).

South Africa has also negotiated a controversial free trade agreement (the Trade Development and Cooperation Agreement) with the European Union, which has meant that it has become a site where the structural power of transnational capital and major world powers is expressed and transmitted throughout the region. This can be potentially developmental. The United Nations Conference on Trade and Development (UNCTAD 2009a) argues that policy-makers in Africa should recognize the important role that TNCs from within Africa and also from other developing countries could play in promoting economic growth. Furthermore, according to Shaw et al. (2009), South African service suppliers in third countries in the rest of Africa may benefit from increasing Chinese mineral demand as they supply throughout the continent.

There is an implicit division of labour under development here, whereby SSA supplies minerals and agricultural raw materials to the outside world, South African companies provide the service infrastructure, and this facilitates China's continuing ascent in the global hierarchy based on manufacturing. In that sense South Africa is serving as a regional conduit or 'courtesan' state for transnational capital (Mittelman 2000), some of which comes increasingly from China. This has facilitated the country's rise to prominence in international fora, such as the BRICS, where it has been noted that 'it's not a natural fit', as its economy is less than a quarter the size of

Russia's and only a little bigger than China's sixth-richest province (Khan, quoted in Herskovitz 2010). Its principal sponsor for accession was China, as 'this is something that China sees in its own interest with its aim of understanding the future of Africa and becoming an even bigger player there' (Zonis, quoted in ibid.). Its attraction to China, in particular, as a partner is partially due to its relative global weakness. Consequently, its bargaining role may limit the extent to which South Africa can genuinely influence global governance regimes so that they are more developmental.

South Africa is the key node for globalized geo-governance in SSA. However, the increasing inequality which is a general feature of globalization (Milanovic 2011) is expressed both domestically within South Africa, and in its relations with the region. This generates both alliances among the beneficiaries of current arrangements – what Sklair (2001) calls the transnational capitalist class – and resistance from subaltern classes. This chapter has explored how South African-based actors, particularly the state and corporations, have promoted geo-governance, or private authority, over resources and markets in SSA. Coordination has been effected through the *embourgeoisement* of the ANC and BEE elite, the construction of a conducive 'liberal' discourse through NEPAD, and direct policies and subsidies. However, this mode of geo-governance is unstable given the inequalities and resistances which it generates.

South Africa's geopolitical strategy in Africa now leverages the power of the Chinese state and influence on the continent. In a sense it could be argued that this is merely a reflection or replication of the strategy behind China's leveraging of the power of Western-dominated international financial institutions to its own ends on the continent. It was these institutions which oversaw the opening up of these economies to foreign trade and investment, to the benefit of Chinese companies in particular, as they have substantial competitive advantages to bring to bear as a consequence of their relationship with the Chinese government. South Africa, then, is now not so much a competitor with China on the continent as a junior partner or 'client state'. This is in contrast to the other BRICS powers, again with the partial exception of Russia, which often view themselves, in some ways or along some dimensions at least, as competitors with China.

4 | INDIA: THE GEO-LOGICS OF AGRO-INVESTMENTS[1]

There is no doubt, that Africa is the New World of the nineteenth century. What America was to Europe in the sixteenth and seventeenth centuries Africa is now. (Harry Johnston, 'British interests in eastern Equatorial Africa', 1885, quoted in Tilley 2011: 31)

There is a sacred tie between the tiller and the land. Any attempt to snap the relationship is bound to face opposition. (Indian Minister of Finance P. Chidambaram, quoted in Shiva 2007)

Buy land. They're not making it anymore. (Mark Twain, quoted in Pearce 2012: vii)

India is a major emerging power of the twenty-first century. This is evidenced by the scale of its economic growth and the rapid growth in overseas engagements. Like South Africa, India has recently set up its own aid agency, with an initial budget of US$15 billion for the first five years of operations (Sunday Guardian 2012). It is also upgrading its military capabilities, recently buying 126 fighter jets from France, for example, and building its own nuclear-powered submarines, partly in response to the perceived growing threat posed by China. Travelling in India, you now see posters boasting of the Indian military's, perhaps overstated, global reach.

In Africa, India has not been, in general, able to bring the same power resources to bear as China. This has resulted in a twin-track strategy of 'globalization slipstreaming' behind China on the continent and cultivation of somewhat diffuse but direct links with African political elites. In Sudan, for example, Indian companies are active, but it is the Chinese who take the brunt of international criticism for their support for the regime by virtue of the scale of their engagement and use of their veto in the UN Security Council to selectively protect the regime. In terms of direct cultivation of links, the Indian govern-ment has sponsored the creation of 'very, very important' people's telecommunications networks, whereby African heads of state can keep in touch and coordinate. As noted earlier, however, there is one area in particular where Indian engagement in Africa is arguably 'out in front' of China's – land. Land is a vitally important resource and also a source of power as it allows people to live.

Food, fuel and life wars

As previous chapters have intimated, there is a second Scramble for Africa now under way (Carmody 2011a). This involves competition over a variety of natural resources from oil to coltan. However, it also involves socio-economic competition over what is perhaps the ultimate resource, as human life is dependent on it – land. Johnston perhaps misread the situation in the nineteenth century in the open-ing quote. The so-called 'New World' in the sixteenth century was composed of two different types of colonies – the 'sugar' colonies of the Caribbean and the 'bread' colonies of mainland North America (Williams 1994). However, in the nineteenth century Africa was valued, by overseas powers at least, for its natural resources and cash crops, primarily, rather than food staples. This is partly changing as land grabbing in Africa is often now for the production of food crops, and also biofuels and other cash crops, for export overseas. This is leading to a reconfiguration of Africa's positionality in the global division of labour, and also the nature of African states.

While the economic dimensions of the land deals which have been concluded in Africa have received substantial media attention, the political dimensions of this process have been less described and ex-plored. This chapter explores the geographic, political and economic motives (geo-logics) behind recent Indian agricultural investments in Africa, with a case study of Ethiopia. It concludes with reflections on what current large-scale foreign land acquisitions mean for the development and trajectory of capitalism on the continent, and the evolution of globalization.

Food prices hit record highs again in 2011: continuing a trend which began to attract global public attention during the price spike of 2007/08 (Bello 2009). There are a variety of reasons for rising prices, including: growth in global population and urbanization, changing consumption patterns in Asia, in particular towards more meat-intensive diets, which require vast quantities of grain and other feedstocks, and financial and land speculation and growth in the usage of biofuels globally (Weiss 2010). So-called first-generation biofuels are often derived from food crops, thereby decreasing supply and driving up prices substantially. The details of this have been explored elsewhere, but it is important to note here that the grain grown for fuel could have fed 330 million people for a year in 2009 (Smith 2010). Sometimes companies also purchase land for biofuels in order to meet carbon compensation or offsetting targets (Zoomers 2011).

High input prices, particularly that of oil, which peaked at over US$147 a barrel in 2008, also drove food prices higher. Dramatically increased prices led to food riots and political unrest in much of the developing world, and several developing countries responded with food export bans, in an attempt to ensure domestic food security. Some countries, such as India, have also encouraged the development by 'their' companies of overseas agricultural investments and food supply chains, which are at least partially autonomous of the vagaries of the global market. According to the vice-president of an Indian bank, the Indian government's ban on non-basmati rice exports drove Indian companies overseas to produce rice for the global market (in GoI Monitor 2011). So large-scale Indian agro-investments abroad are also partly a function of capital accumulation, rather than food security, concerns. However, national 'double movements', whereby society and the polity attempt to re-embed the market after it has largely escaped regulation (Polanyi 1944), as expressed through the export ban in India, for example, are not necessarily progressive in their impacts in the context of globalization as described below.

The trajectory of land deals overseas follows the global power gradient. Between 2004 and 2009 Ethiopia, Ghana, Madagascar, Mali and Sudan allocated land greater than double the size of the UK to foreign investors (Smith 2010). Dramatic increases in food prices mean many more people around the world are now malnourished, so the current global 'food security regime' is failing (Nally 2011a). However, agro-investments overseas may, paradoxically, contribute to increased hunger in the localities in which they are situated. What are the motivations and impacts of Indian agro-investments in Africa, and how do they shed light on these global trends?

The geo-logics of Indian land grabbing in Africa

Indian trade with Africa is booming, amounting to US$45 billion in 2010/11, by some estimates, and increasing by 400 per cent in the last five years (Noury 2012). In 2006 India acquired 12 per cent of its gold imports, 79 per cent of its phosphates, 91 per cent of its nuts and 16 per cent of its copper from the continent (Naidu 2009). Nine out of every ten rough diamonds around the world are cut and polished in India and they are the country's single largest export, at around US$14 billion a year (AsiaPulse News 2008). Of the US$10 billion in rough diamonds imported each year into India, around 80 per cent are thought to come from Africa. Its African trade is argu-ably of greater strategic importance to India than China's, given the structure of trade between the two and the importance of particular commodities such as diamonds, gold, cashew nuts and now food crops, in addition to oil and other minerals, also important to China (Carmody 2011b).

Trade in agricultural products between the two regions is becom-ing increasingly important, and this is also driving new forms of investment. In the wake of the global food price crisis an Indian government committee recommended that Indian companies should be encouraged to shop 'for land abroad for growing crops to meet consumption needs' (Hooda Committee, quoted in Rowden 2011: 16). Twelve per cent of investment by Indian companies in Africa is now in the 'food, beverages and tobacco' sector (Barka and Mlambo 2011).

The import of edible oils is the second largest drain on India's foreign exchange after crude oil. The situation is even more critical in the case of pulses (lentils), which provide most Indians their protein component of their food. Official estimates project that India's pulses production will increase from around 14.86 million tons in 2009–2010 to around 15.73 million tons in 2011–12 (a 6 percent increase). But demand for pulses is expected to rise faster from 18.29 million tons in 2009–10 to around 19.91 million tons in 2011–2012 (9%). Increasing population and the reduction of poverty are both likely to contribute to demand rising faster than these official estimates. (Rowden 2011: 9)

These trends are incentivizing Indian offshore agro-investments. However, land deals are infused with multiple political and economic agendas and logics making them 'polymorphous crystallizations' (Mann 1986).

Grabbing is defined by the *Oxford English Dictionary* as seizing something quickly. While land grabbing in Africa has received a lot of attention in the last couple of years, it has a long history in India (Gadgil and Guha 1995). Recently, there has been substantial controversy around the practice of grabbing land for the development of special economic zones in that country, although the land parcels involved are relatively modest in size when compared to recent land purchases and leases in Africa (Basu 2007).

On the 'push' side of the equation, one factor driving the overseas expansion of Indian agro-corporations is declining groundwater tables in northern and central India (Rowden 2011). These pressures are likely to intensify, as according to the US National Intelligence Director, 'for India, our research indicates the practical effects of climate change will be manageable by New Delhi through 2030. Beyond 2030, India's ability to cope will be reduced by declining agricultural productivity, decreasing water supplies, and increasing pressures from cross-border migration into the country' (quoted in Parenti 2011: 139).

Differential production costs also pull investment to Africa. 'The cost of agricultural production in Africa is almost half that in India. There is less need for fertilizer and pesticides, labour is cheap and overall output is higher,' according to a director of the Indian Lucky Group (quoted in Rowden 2011: 11). Indian investors can lease 60 acres in Africa for the price of what it would cost to lease one acre in the Punjab (*Indian Express*, in GoI 2011), and the availability of contiguous landholdings is also a major advantage, as 'with a per capita holding of 1.5 acres in Punjab, agriculture is ceasing to be a sustainable activity' (Vashisht 2010, quoted in Rowden 2011: 11). As labour is also 'cheap' in India, it is land cost and availability which are decisive.

There are a number of paradoxes at the heart of Indian efforts to source land in Africa. According to Parenti (2011: 143), in India 'irrigation has suffered under a wave of neoliberal disinvestment. The state has removed important subsidies from small farmers; as a result, thousands of them have killed themselves', even as Indian agro-conglomerates expand overseas. The current process of agrarian restructuring in India has been described as 'immiserizing growth', as agricultural output rises but incomes fall (Vakulabharanam, quoted in ibid.: 147). Approximately 47 per cent of Indian children are malnourished. So why is there such concern to source food in Africa, when domestic food security was not a priority during the era of economic liberalization from 1991 in that country? This points to the importance of capital and other economic logics in the overseas expansion.

To maintain its recent 8 per cent average economic growth rate India needs to increase its primary energy supply by three to four times its 2003/04 levels (Naidu 2010). It is also estimated that India will run out of coal in the next forty years. Consequently it currently needs, and will increasingly need, to import the majority of its energy needs, and it is projected that by 2030 India may be the world's third-largest consumer of energy after the United State and China (Naidu 2009). India now imports 11 per cent of its oil from Africa, partly to fuel its rapidly growing car fleet (Arnold 2009). In the capital of India, Delhi, alone, an extra 200,000 cars are added to the streets every year (Shiva 2008).

Given its rapidly increasing demand for energy, India launched a National Mission on Biodiesel in 2003 (Smith 2010). In order to meet national biofuel production targets India needs to plant, or gain access to, an area roughly equivalent to that used for all farming in the UK by 2016/17, with *Jatropha curcas* – a tree from which biofuel can be produced (ibid.). However, this has encountered domestic resistance as local communities insisted on being given title to government-owned forest and wasteland before they would participate, and owners of marginal lands were not willing to grow jatropha unless given assured returns (ibid.). This, however, means that part of this demand can be exported to countries such as Ethiopia, where democracy is not an issue. This means that 'many of these Indian companies operating in Africa are engaging in activities that involve huge displacement of farmers and changing patterns of production and consumption that would either be difficult or impossible for them to do in India. They would either be illegal or get embroiled in very significant political controversies because of the negative impact on local people' (Ghosh 2011), thus illustrating the tension between corporate capitalism and electoral democracy. However, the Indian government is keen to encourage this overseas investment trend and has facilitated land investments overseas, through a $640 million line of credit from its Export-Import (Exim) bank to Ethiopia for the Tindaho Sugar Project, for example (GoI Monitor 2011). Sugar can be used to produce ethanol (a biofuel). The Indian government also gave the Economic Community of West African States a quarter of a billion dollars to establish a fund to promote biofuels (Smith 2010).

Biofuels are meant to be a carbon-neutral or positive 'fix' for the ecological contradiction between fixed amounts of terrestrial resources and an ever-expanding global economy (O'Connor 1994). By accessing energy from the sun more directly through plant life they present themselves as an extra-global fix to this dilemma. However, when the carbon costs of land clearance are also included in the analysis this often turns out not to be the case, as the sink resources of the global atmosphere and oceans are further depleted.

Land grabbing and climate change have profound direct and in-direct impacts for many of the poor in Africa. For example, the United Nations Intergovernmental Panel on Climate Change estimates that the value of African crops could fall by up to 90 per cent by the turn of the century as a result of anthropogenically induced climate change (Toulmin 2009).[2] Other estimates suggest that the value of crops could fall by 50 per cent as early as 2020. Land grabbing has implications for the pace of climate change as land conversion, noted above, often results in the release of carbon through forest clearance and burning, and new land uses are often far less effective in carbon sequestration. For example, according to one author of a report on the development of biofuel plantations, 'the clearance of grassland released 93 times the amount of greenhouse gases that would be saved by the fuel made annually on that land' (Fargione, quoted in Shiva 2008: 80), thus actually accelerating the pace of climate change. One of the countries which has attracted the most Indian agro-investments in Africa is Ethiopia, to which we now turn.

Seeing like an (under)developmental state? The political logic and impacts of Indian land grabbing in Ethiopia

According to Philip McMichael (1997: 645), 'rather than conceive of globalisation phenomenally, as a trend, it is more usefully conceived of as a contradictory historical project – a mechanism of political and economic restructuring'. The question is, for whose benefit is it undertaken?

Seventy per cent of foreign investment in agricultural land in Ethiopia is by Indian companies (Gebremedhin 2011). The most controversial of these deals has featured Karuturi, the world's largest producer of cut roses, which it had previously started growing in Ethiopia. The company sells about 650 million stems a year (Pearce 2012). It has been pledged access to 800,000 acres of land on lease by the Ethiopian government for food and other crops (Rugman 2012), with a rent of US$1.18 per hectare for the first 100,000 hectares, compared to an average of around $360 a year in India (Ghosh 2011). If the investment proceeds as planned and is completed it will be the largest farm in Africa. The initial lease is for fifty years. There are no performance conditions, such as producing food for the domestic market, attached to these contracts, and because much of the production is highly mechanized they result in substantial labour displacement. According to one estimate, expected 'job creation' is only 0.005 per hectare, or 500 jobs per 100,000 hectares (Gebremedhin 2011). By way of comparison, South Africa is one of the world's top ten wine producers, but all of the country's grapes for wine are produced on around 100,000 hectares.

In fact, rather than having conditions attached, the Ethiopian government has incentivized these investments through exemptions from tax and import duties on inputs, and no restrictions on land and water use. According to one Indian agriculturalist in Gambella working for Karuturi: 'You can grow anything here; the climate is ideal. We have no land like this in India. There we are lucky to get 1 per cent organic matter in the soil. Here it is more than 5 per cent. We don't even need fertilizer. All for an annual rent of about a dollar a hectare' (quoted in Pearce 2012: 8).

Ethiopia is known as the 'water tower' of East Africa (Demmissie 2011). Consequently this is as much 'virtual water' (Allan 1998), whereby water is used to produce agricultural commodities for export, as a land grab. The Ethiopian government does, however, collect land transfer costs of around $35 per hectare on the land, so there is a substantial monetary advantage arising from this.

According to the Ethiopian minister for agriculture, 'we give land because we cannot produce on that land. Because of lack of capital and technology, that's why. They open a big opportunity for employment and of course generation of taxes and other financial gain' (quoted in Rugman 2012). This gain also applies for the Indian companies, so political and economic logics articulate to generate new forms of dispossession and exclusion. On the demand side food imports are incentivized as Ethiopian farm produce entering the country is now taxed less than domestic produce, according to an official of the Federation of Indian Export Organizations (Rowden 2011).

In terms of biofuel investments, states are sometimes keen to promote these in order to gain access to energy supplies, particularly given recent high oil prices (Ness et al. 2009). However, there are livelihood implications as water in Ethiopia for food crops is diverted to biofuel irrigation systems (Meinzen-Dick 2010, in Matondi 2011). Other impacts include loss of access to land, grazing rights, wood, other ecosystem products such as meat, and loss of personal worth and sense of belonging (Matondi 2011).

What does the Ethiopian case tell us about the nature of the state in that country and how Indian engagement is changing it? Is the state developmental, predatory or hybrid ([under]developmental)? (Evans 1995).

There are clear financial incentives around the transnational contract of extraversion (Carmody 2010), whereby the Ethiopian state gets tax revenues and hard currency earnings from allying itself with foreign corporations. But in the Ethiopian case these are mostly used for developmental purposes, in contrast to the situation in many other states in Africa (Radelet 2010). This relates to the political economy of that country, as the Ethiopian government is dominated by the minority Tigrayan ethnic group, which was the target of a genocide under the previous regime (Meredith 2005), and this expenditure is important to attain acquiescence among the population more broadly and to secure continuing aid inflows to bolster the regime. Ethiopia is the largest recipient of aid in Africa and, remarkably, the third largest in the world. In 2008 aid amounted to 13 per cent of gross national income and the equivalent of 133 per cent of general government expenditure (Fengler and Kharas 2010). However, the constitution of state hegemony also involves force and some interesting ideological manoeuvres.

According to the former prime minister of Ethiopia, Meles Zenawi (2011: 140), 'the neoliberal paradigm is a dead end incapable of bringing about an African Renaissance'. However, in terms of the shift in agricultural policy away from smallholder agriculture, current developments in Ethiopia would appear to fit with the neoliberal approach. For example:

> carefully analysing the World Development Report 2008, Kjell Havnevik and his associates see the new World Bank paradigm for African agriculture as one based on the rapid development of contract and corporate farming. Smallholders are seen as largely non-competitive, and the thrust of agricultural policy is to facilitate their conversion into large-scale contract farmers or workers for corporate farms. WDR 2008, in short, 'is recommending global capital's destruction of an independent smallholder agricultural sector'. (Havenevik et al. 2008, quoted in Bello 2009: 82)

In Ethiopia the economic logic as elaborated by the former prime minister was that 'developing countries cannot compete solely on the basis of factor endowments or by buying up the latest machinery. They need to assimilate technology developed elsewhere, and they need to continuously move up the technology ladder if they are to achieve continued growth and development' (Meles 2011: 163). However, there has been virtually no technology transfer in relation to agro-investment (Rahmato 2011), so there must be other logics at play.

Land allocations are part of a general drive to attract foreign investment from India, which increased to US$4.7 billion in the space of four years. According to the former prime minister, who died in office in 2012, 'We want to see more Indian companies in every field, from textiles and food processing to IT [information technology] and agriculture' (Meles, quoted in Rowden 2011: 14).

There are more than thirty-five Indian companies active in land deals in Ethiopia, and some government officials estimate that half of all land being allocated to foreign investors will be allocated to them. The amounts of land being allocated are substantial – estimated at 38 per cent of the land area currently being used by smallholders in that country (Rahmato 2011). According to the Ethiopian agriculture minister: 'How much land will actually go to Indian investors depends entirely on the interest of investors. If they come and take *all* the land, then we will be very happy' (quoted in Rowden 2011: 14, emphasis added). Prime Minister Meles was somewhat more measured, explaining 'there is no land grab ... We have three million hectares of unutilised land. This is land not used by anybody' (quoted in ibid.: 14). However, this may not be the case, as land which appears 'unused' from the 'god's eye' view provided by satellite imagery may simply be in long-fallow cultivation cycles as a result of the fragility of the soils (Von Braun and Meinzen-Dick 2009, in ibid.).

Satellite imagery now serves the function of old explorers' maps, and the colonial idea of uninhabited land (*terra nullius*) which could be claimed by overseas 'investors' is being implicitly rehabilitated. This colonial mind-set is certainly in evidence among Indian state elites as globalization is reconfiguring the nature of sovereignty so that it is more liminal and porous (Harrison 2005). When the first shipment of oil from Sudan from India's state-owned oil company arrived by supertanker in Mangalore in 2003, the Indian deputy prime minister declared, 'this is not imported oil, this is India's oil' (quoted in Oil and Gas Journal 2003, in Patey 2011: 88). Could this logic be extended so that land being purchased by Indian companies in Africa is now considered by Indian political elites as 'Indian land'?

The scale of the relocation programme in Ethiopia is vast; with 42 per cent of Gambella region's land earmarked by the government for investment and overall plans to relocate 1.5 million people across four of the country's regions (Oakland Institute, cited in Kemenade 2012). This is despite, or perhaps because of, the previous disastrous experience with villagization in Ethiopia (Scott 1998). Villagization programmes across Africa have been notoriously difficult as concentration of population often leads to intensified soil erosion in what are often easily degraded fragile environments. However, they do have sound political and economic logics.

Parts of Ethiopia are chronically food insecure and famines are profoundly political events that have sometimes been induced for political ends, as was the case in Ethiopia in the 1980s (Meredith 2005). Food and access to the means of subsistence (land) are fundamental biopolitical questions which govern the quality, and indeed the existence, of life itself (Nally 2011b) in largely agrarian societies. Consequently control over access to food and land could be regarded as the ultimate form of political power.

The resettlements are taking place in regions outside of Tigray Province, from which the ruling elite in Ethiopia come. While the World Bank has recommended privatization of land in Ethiopia, the government has resisted this, as it would compromise a major source of political power. Thus foreign investors have been granted land rights in Ethiopia which are denied to citizens (Demmissie 2011). By displacing these people into a villagization programme they can be more easily politically controlled, ensuring the Tigrayan People's Liberation Front/Ethiopian People's Revolutionary Democratic Front's (EPRDF) continued grip on power (Rahmato 2011). This mirrors other strategies pursued by the EPRDF to stay in power (see Carmody 2007), and the geo-logic of spatial and biopolitical control interacts with private sector economic logics. Tigrayan settlers have also been given substantial land holdings in Gambella, for example (Pearce 2012).

There is an irony that it is former 'socialist' states such as China and Ethiopia which are able to provide conditions most conducive to inward investment, because of their greater control over the other factors of production; particularly land and labour. In the Ethiopian case, state ownership of land makes population displacement relatively easy, with an estimated 70,000 people displaced in Gambella province alone in 2011 (Human Rights Watch, cited in Kemenade 2012). According to this report, security forces 'repeatedly threatened, assaulted, and arrested villagers' who resisted relocation. The process was also associated with rape, burning down of homes and killing of cattle. The new villages to which people were relocated report- edly lacked farmland, food and health infrastructure. The minister for agriculture in Ethiopia was very forthright about the Ethiopian poor's lack of usufruct land rights. According to him, 'pastoralists displaced by land grabbing "can just go somewhere else"' (quoted in Palmer 2010: 5, in Matondi et al. 2011: 5). This also has echoes of colonialism.

The English political economist George Scrope considered that British government policy had made the Irish peasantry 'human encumbrances', which others in policy circles felt the Great Famine in Ireland would sweep away, thus allowing for agricultural mod- ernization (Nally 2011c). In the lease agreement with Karuturi the Ethiopian government is required to hand over leased land 'free of impediments'. 'Arguably local people who are unwilling to leave their land could be construed as "impediments" and the lessor is now contractually obligated to ensure they are not a problem for the company' (Rowden 2011: 30). The government also undertakes to provide 'security' for these investments, and the government of Gambella told locals that resistance to such investments would be considered 'anti-development' (in ibid.: 26), perfectly illustrating James Ferguson's (1990) thesis on how the discourse of development can be used to obscure oppressive power relations.

According to a farmer displaced by the Karuturi investment in Ethiopia, 'when they first came they told us an investor was com- ing and we would develop the land alongside one another. They didn't say the land would be taken away from us entirely. I don't understand why the government took the land (Gemechu, cited in Rugman 2012). His spouse noted, 'since the land was taken away from us we are impoverished. Nothing has gone right for us since these investors came.' However, the dispossession has a profound disciplinary effect in Ethiopia as large-scale land acquisitions serve as 'a constant reminder of the danger hanging over small farmers and pastoralists and their way of life' (Rahmato 2011: 5), thus creating a new land (in)security regime.

Peasant resistance in Ethiopia has included 'encroachments on land given out to investment projects, driving livestock to graze on them, disputing boundary limits, taking one's grievances to court, or appealing to higher authorities for redress of grievances' (ibid.: 17), with some success based on an intervention by the Ethiopian president in one case. However, global forces through their structural power often prevail.

India's Exim bank is expected to facilitate the Karuturi investment in Ethiopia, for example, and shareholders in the company include the Boston-based Sandstone Capital (Rowden 2011). On the 600,000 hectares currently leased to foreign investors in Ethiopia about 20,000 jobs are meant to be created; however, many more people may have been displaced in the process. Furthermore, some of the land used to produce teff, the staple food in Ethiopia, now produces maize for export, perhaps contributing to recent price increases for teff. At the Karuturi investment many of the labourers are reportedly children or adults who are paid 70 US cents a day, which is less than what people earn in Ethiopia's minimalist 'Productive Safety Net Programme'.

Gambella is thought to host the second-largest wildlife migration in the world (Rahmato 2011), consisting of a variety of large mammals such as antelope, and this may be disrupted by the land acquisitions. In Rahmato's study people also recounted how they survived drought by collecting roots and other edible plants in the forest, but when the forest was cleared this was no longer possible. The Karuturi investment also resulted in the clearance of an Anuak burial ground.

Mono-agricultures are environmentally unsustainable and, according to Vandana Shiva (2008: 2), 'the food crisis reflects a deeper crisis – the creation of "redundant" or disposable people and, alongside them, the potential for violence and social and political instability'. However, there is another reading, which is that large agro-investments generate their own, and create a reserve, 'army' of labour. Even if the arguments about them generating employment are accepted, according to calculations in a World Bank report, a smallholder farmer in Zambia could make six times more producing sugar cane than earning wages working on the same crop (Murray Li 2011). Rather, 'investors cannot be responsible for poverty reduction: an impoverished population surrounding a plantation is the ideal situation for maximum profit. The last thing a plantation company needs is for the surrounding population to prosper' (ibid.: 291). Indeed, there is an internal logic as population displacement, often from very 'cheap' land, also creates a 'cheap' labour force.

Under Ethiopian government policy, income from land deals is meant to be utilized for the benefit of the regions involved, unless the land is transferred into the federal land bank, and there has been pressure from the central regime to do this. Regional leaders tend to comply with central government wishes as they often find themselves in jail if they do not (Samatar 2004). The central Ethiopian government gets access to land fees, taxes and export revenue, and the economy has grown by more than 10 per cent a year since 2004, giving a doubling time of less than seven years. However, some of the peasantry pay the price, even as Ethiopia's aggregate position in the Global Hunger Index improves (Deutsche Welthungerhilfe et al. 2011).

Some might argue there are certain relative advantages to Indian agro-investments in Africa. For example, Chinese companies have often been criticized for bringing substantial portions of their labour force from China. One of the conditions of a multibillion-dollar loan to the government of Angola was that 70 per cent of the works associated with new contracts should go to Chinese companies, for example. In contrast, stated Indian policy is different. When the Indian vice-president toured Africa he noted:

> The direction in which the Indian economy is going, the major role will be played by the private sector, especially in industrial development. Local employment will be generated. It doesn't make economic sense to take work-force from India because it comes with liabilities. When we go for an investment venture, we don't go with the idea of imposing our work-force or employment of Indians *per se*. We seek to limit ourselves to management and financial control of enterprises having an Indian element. (Quoted in Naidu 2011: 64)

However, the generation of employment by these agro-investments is small and comes with a high 'opportunity cost' and substantial human suffering, and there are reports that Karuturi may now outsource 20,000 hectares of land in Ethiopia to Indian farmers on a revenue-sharing basis (Badrinath 2011).

(Re)globalizing the underdevelopment of capitalism in Africa

Colonialism in Africa can be considered a 'round of globalization', oriented towards providing raw materials and markets for metropolitan European powers. However, 'at the time of decolonization in the '60s, Africa was not just self-sufficient in food but was actually a net food exporter, averaging [a modest] 1.3 million tons in food exports a year between 1966 and 1970. Today, the continent imports 25 percent of its food, with almost every country being a net food importer' (Bello 2009: 68).

The global land grab is a feature of the current round of globalization related to the deepening commoditization of land (Zoomers 2010). However, the double movement, whereby society reacts against commoditization, fails to operate in the context of globalization as might be expected. Rather we are witnessing the involution of globalization – or a new double movement – whereby market actors seeks to circumvent markets owing to their instability, establishing dedicated supply chains for inputs. New global agro-investments which commodify land often 'aim not to serve the international markets, but rather to circumvent them, by tightening the control of investors from the place of production to the end consumer' (De Schutter 2011: 253). This is a response to the system of organized entropy (Carmody 2011c) constituted by global capitalism and represents a partial decommodification of food in response to its special properties – its implicit biopower – for those who control it. It also suggests we need to differentiate between fixed and mobile flows of globalization, as the global economy is founded on natural resources found in specific places which are not subject to 'liquification' (Ritzer 2010). Rather, the power relations surrounding them seem to be subject to securitization or solidification, as the Ethiopian case demonstrates.

In relation to land grabbing, according to German et al. (2011: 1), 'governments are playing an active role – often bolstered by an unwavering faith in the role of foreign investment in national economic development'. This ideology fits with government interests in the process as they derive tax revenues, exports and foreign currency, ancillary benefits and disciplinary power, all of which serve to strengthen regime survival. Part of these revenues may be invested in developmental expenditures to generate consent, as in Ethiopia. In addition, as many of the land deals are non-transparent, kickbacks may also play a part in the process. What is the potential for reform?

Recently there has been discussion of compulsory or voluntary codes of conduct around global land grabbing. However, these have failed to gain traction at the Food and Agriculture Organization of the UN for political reasons. Furthermore, proposals for a code of conduct around land deals do not address structural issues or challenge existing unsustainable global industrial energy and agro-food complexes (Borras and Franco n.d.). The colonial legacy in Africa also ends up reproducing colonial-style relations in the current land grab. For example, in Zambia all land is vested in the president – making land allocation to foreign investors easy.

In an important article Professor John Sender (1999) defined himself as a 'tragic optimist' in relation to the progressive potential of capitalist developmental states in Africa. However, the embracing of the supposedly post-neoliberal 'Chinese' model of development on the continent implies the creation of oligopolistic political economies in which political elites hold substantial personal stakes (Taylor 2010, in Cornelissen et al. 2011). This is certainly the case in Ethiopia, where privatization has been to the benefit of EPRDF elites, which helps generate funds to cement political control. Large-scale land acquisitions also serve to discipline the rural population. However, neither privatization nor the new enclosure movement promotes industrialization as profits flow offshore in the latter case, rather than being reinvested domestically, as in Britain after the first enclosure movement, where they helped promote the Industrial Revolution.

In his seminal work De Janvry (1981) identified two primary paths to agrarian development – the 'farmer road' and the Junker one, named for the large-scale landed-gentry class in Prussia in the nineteenth century. These different paths and approaches are still evident in Africa today. For example, major progress has been made in Malawi in achieving food security and generating food exports through a programme of subsidy provision of fertilizer and other input 'starter packs' to small-scale farmers (Denning et al. 2009). In contrast some have argued that Ethiopia is witnessing a 'South Africanization' of its agrarian structure, as large-scale land enclosure takes place; implying greater inequality. Which of these paths is pursued is fundamentally a political question.

The impacts of large-scale agro-investments are also not pre-determined, but depend on local conditions, such as pre-existing land uses, government policies and the ways in which they are implemented. For example, Boamah (2011) shows how a biodiesel project in northern Ghana diversified local livelihoods and thereby increased local food security, in the short term. The intercropping of food with biofuel also provided some support for the idea of 'vent for surplus'; that cash crops need not necessarily displace food crops if there are unused resources. However, the project which he describes ultimately failed as a result of the global financial crisis, showing how these projects increase risk for locals by helping create translocalities (Appadurai 1995), which are deeply exposed to global processes. According to James Smith (2010), whatever the benefits of biofuels, they globalize risk and perpetuate inequality and existing unsustainable consumption patterns.

Large-scale agro-projects create both local and globalized risks for local people, contributing to the further development of the 'risk society' (Beck 1992) and increasing vulnerability, and often poverty. They represent forms of 'accumulation by dispossession' (Harvey 2003), which increase inequality and store up further sources of conflict for the future – an 'economy of disaffection'. The deputy director of the Food and Agriculture Organization argued that we could 'imagine empty trucks being driven into, say, Ethiopia, at the time of food shortages caused by war or drought, and being driven out again, full of grain to feed people overseas ... Can you imagine the consequences of that?' (quoted in Rowden 2011: 8).

Mega-projects often generate resistance. For example, the Merowe dam in Sudan, which was funded and built by Chinese and Middle Eastern loans and built by Chinese and European companies, resulted in approximately 70,000 people being displaced and the Sudanese government shooting protesters dead. However, as intimated above, large-scale 'land grabs' which are even more spatially extensive have the potential to be even more politically explosive in the medium term.

Many of the largest Chinese companies active in Africa are partially state owned, and therefore their actions reflect back on the state. Consequently, while they have to be somewhat careful and mindful of public relations, this is less true for privately owned or publicly traded Indian conglomerates. However, the Indian government is still keen to support their overseas expansion in order to facilitate domestic economic growth and other strategic objectives, around food supply, for example. While there have been a number of outbreaks of 'anti-Chinese' rioting and violence in Africa, and in Zambia in particular, the growing politicization of land and resistance to land grabs may also result in violence directed against the Indian presence on the continent in the future.

5 | RUSSIA: UNALLOYED SELF-INTEREST OR REFLECTIONS IN THE MIRROR?

Russia is far behind Western and Chinese companies when it comes to securing a share of the continent's [Africa's] natural wealth. (BBC 2009b)

And what does Ireland gain from this? (Senior Russian official to former head of Irish Aid, quoted in Murphy 2012: 14)

There are three main schools in international relations: realist, liberal institutionalist and constructivist. The premise of realist theory is that the international system is inherently anarchic and that states pursue power politics to further their own (security) interests. Liberal institutionalists, in contrast, focus on the way in which states cooperate to achieve common goals, such as the creation of trade agreements to facilitate economic growth. Social constructivists, on the other hand, argue that interests are not preordained, but constructed (Wendt 1999). More recently work has been done on the way in which emotion, rather than interests – narrowly defined – influences geopolitics (Moisi 2009). This chapter argues that both emotion and more classical economic and political 'interests' have intertwined in Russia's renewed engagement in Africa.

The fall and rise of Russia

In order to understand the geopolitical code (Kraxberger 2005) whereby the Russian state or policy elites rank and assign importance to a particular place, and the position of Africa within this, it is necessary to understand recent Russian history. According to the political scientist Peter Rutland (2012), twenty years after the collapse of the Soviet Union, Russian foreign policy still lacks a sense of direction. One poll conducted in 2003 found that when given a choice between being a Great Power (*derzhava*) or having a high standard of living, 43 per cent of Russians chose the former (New Russia Barometer 2003, cited in ibid.).

The economic and geopolitical collapse of the 1990s was experienced by the majority of Russians as a national humiliation. President Vladimir Putin has referred to the fact that Russians subtly feel Africa's problems. Perhaps one of these problems is the relative lack of respect which had previously been accorded to both in international relations. The post-Soviet turmoil of Russia led one Western observer to describe the country as 'Zaire with permafrost' (Larson and Shevchenko 2010).

Russia has experienced dramatic swings in fortune over the last twenty-five years. It is the only country in the world that has gone from being a superpower, to an aid recipient, to being an aid donor again (Gray n.d.), and once more a 'great', if somewhat diminished, power. Vladimir Putin, recently re-elected in disputed circumstances, as Russia's president, previously spoke of the collapse and break-up of the Soviet Union as the 'greatest geopolitical catastrophe of the twentieth century' (quoted in Bouzarovksi and Bassin 2011: 788). Since coming to power in 2000 for two terms as president, and subsequently as prime minister, and then again as president, he has viewed the revival of Russian power as his foremost foreign policy goal.[1] This has been expressed in a variety of ways, from armed conflict with Georgia over South Ossetia, to the assertive claims to Arctic resources, to Russian military aircraft 'buzzing' Icelandic airspace since the closure of the American military base in that country in 2006, as the US focus shifted to Iraq and Afghanistan. More recently the United States Agency for International Development has been expelled from the country over allegations of interference in the presidential election, and a law has been passed banning American adoption of Russian children, in response to a US law imposing sanctions on human rights abusers from Russia.

According to Rutland there are three levels of interaction in the international system: military, economic, and culture and identity. 'It is in the *vexed* area of cultural identity that the uncertainties wrought by the transformations in the military and economic realms come together' (Rutland 2012: 3, emphasis in original). Thus there is no neat separation between identity and economic interests.

Arguably the political opportunity structure in Russia has favoured the emergence of 'strongmen' who can govern a sprawling multinational state. However, the political opportunity structure which confronted Vladimir Putin, in particular, on his assumption of power in 2000 favoured him prioritizing the resurgence of Russian international prestige or Great Power status. Great Powers, as opposed to middle powers, are defined by their global reach, interest and influence, and Russian (re-)engagement in Africa should be read in that light. The resurgence of Great Power status would also serve to consolidate domestic sovereignty, and in order to understand Russia's re-engagement in Africa, it is necessary to understand the political economy of that country.

'Poor governance is the rule of men [and women], not law' (Yates 2012). Vladimir Putin's Russia is characterized by 'soft' authoritarianism, even if he 'legitimately' won the plurality of votes in his 2012 re-election. In its 2012 annual report, Freedom House (2012) rates the Russian press as having the same level of freedom as Zimbabwe's. Many journalists in Russia have been assassinated under Putin and Medvedev's rule, and the owner of Russia's largest oil company, Yukos, was imprisoned for tax evasion and the assets of the company mostly sold to the Russian state. According to Kimmage (2009: 51):

> Russia under the current regime can be described as a selectively capitalist kleptocracy because it employs certain genuine components of a market economy, but only to the extent that they benefit, or at the very least do not hinder, a ruling elite engaged in practices that would entail criminal prosecution in any free-market society with a functioning legal system and an independent judiciary. These practices include outright theft of budgetary funds, pervasive graft and kickbacks on all major contracts, myriad tax-evasion schemes, and a welter of unfair business tactics based on influence-peddling, access to insider information, and the manipulation of ambiguous laws and pliant courts.

Accusations of graft can also serve political ends. The value of shares of Mechel, one of Russia's biggest mining and metals companies, fell nearly $6 billion in a single day when Putin made a remark suggesting the company's chief executive had engaged in shady dealings (Kramer 2008). Little wonder Forbes listed him in 2011 as the world's second-most powerful person, after Barack Obama

(Forbes 2011b).[2] While the precise definition of authoritarianism can be debated, as can whether or not it applies to Putin's Russia, it is certainly a 'strong state', domestically at least.

Russian foreign policy in the Putin era has undergone an important set of evolutions. In the early 2000s, according to one report, the Russians, 'with American support, are attempting nothing less than to replace OPEC [Organization of the Petroleum Exporting Countries] as the world's major supplier of energy' (Jane's Foreign Report 2002). In 2001, Putin's adviser Andrei Illarionov argued that OPEC was an 'historically doomed organization' (Katz 2001, quoted in Bukkvoll 2003: 232). However, Putin's initial reorientation towards the West was strategic and relations have since cooled. 'Until recently, Russia saw itself as Pluto in the Western solar system, very far from the centre but still fundamentally a part of it. Now it has left that orbit entirely: Russian leaders have given up on becoming part of the West and have started creating their own Moscow-centred system' (Trenin 2006). In terms of voting at the United Nations, Kim and Russett (1996) found that Russia occupied an intermediate position on the North–South axis: voting with different blocs depending on the issue. While China is a 'rising power', and consequently feels the need not to alienate potential developing country allies around the world, Russia's self-image and representation are arguably as a 'Great Power' which does not have to be as concerned with this, as evidenced by its invasion of South Ossetia in 2008.

In part, the drift of Russia away from the West was the result of American attempts under the neoconservative regime of George W. Bush to aggressively assert dominance in international affairs (Kiely 2005). Now that Russia's economy has been resuscitated on the back of energy exports, Putin is attempting to achieve economic transformation to further build the power of the Russian state and ensure acquiescence to his rule domestically.

Internationally there are a variety of vectors or channels through which Russian Great Power status could be reasserted, for example through selectively challenging the USA's positions in international relations, over the invasion of Iraq, for example.[3] Great Power status can also be displayed through the opulence of the leader. A recent report revealed that Vladimir Putin has access to fifty-eight aircraft, worth an estimated billion dollars, with the fittings on his Ilyushin jet costing more than a hundred million pounds sterling, and twenty holiday homes (one of which alone is worth almost a billion US dollars) (Parfitt 2012). However, the primary modality was through the construction of Russia as an 'energy superpower' (*energeticheskaia sverkhderzhava*); a vector which has been extended to other parts of the world, such as Africa.

According to Ronald Hill (2008: 476, citing Jowitt 2008), 'Putin's vision for Russia is of a strong state that is served by the nation, and a nation that is in turn served by the state in a symbiotic kind of relationship. At the present stage of development, Putin functions as a Patriot-King – even though such a political style "prevents the emergence not only of citizens but also politicians". In that case, the long-term destiny of Russia is uncertain.' In an attempt to pre-empt the contradictions of this mode of rule, on his re-election in 2012 Vladimir Putin set out an ambitious agenda to transform Russia into a high-tech economy. Some argue that this may mean that oligarchs are forced to invest in these sectors and that Russian high-tech products may be exported to Africa, as they are unlikely to be initially competitive elsewhere (Damina Advisors 2012). Also, the shock of the oil price collapse from nearly US$150 a barrel to US$50 a barrel as a result of the global financial crisis gave added impetus to diversification of the Russian economy, although this had always been Putin's plan. For him the energy sector would be 'the major catalyst for the modernisation and qualitative development of the entire economy of the Russian Federation' (Putin, quoted in Bouzarovski and Bassin 2011: 790).

Russia is geographically adjacent to Europe and Asia; two of the most populous regions of the world, but which lack sufficient domestic energy sources to meet their current requirements (ibid.). In fact Russia supplies Europe with almost a quarter of its oil and gas. This has given the Russian state substantial geopolitical leverage, and Vladimir Putin reportedly wrote a PhD thesis on natural resource management in the 1990s.[4] According to the director of Russia's National Energy Security Foundation, energy is the ultimate strategic weapon, as once it is denied to competitors 'the geopolitical struggle is won' (Simonov 2006).

Between 1998 and 2004 48 per cent of the increase in world oil supply came from Russia (Tomson and Ahrend 2006, cited in Rutland 2008). In 2009 it cut off gas supplies to Europe after a pricing dispute with Ukraine. One strategy which Putin pursued to cement his own power was the effective renationalization of the energy sector in Russia at the start of the 2000s. However, many of Russia's major oil and gas fields – the primary source of Russia's renewed wealth and geopolitical influence – are in decline. From the mid-1990s to 2000 the production of the Samotlor oilfield declined by five-sixths and the Romashkino field by two-thirds from 1970 to 2000 (Moyo 2012). This is a primary driver of Russia's re-engagement with Africa.

Africa is playing an increasingly important role in Russia's geo-political code, serving three primary interrelated functions in this: 1) representational – as a place where Russia can assert its claim to be a 'Great Power' and as a site through which the idea of Russia is (re)constructed; 2) as a source of diplomatic support and prestige for Russia in the United Nations and other international arenas; 3) as a place of opportunity and expansion for Russian corporations through direct investment and exports.

The history of Afro-Russian relations

Russia, and its predecessor state, the Soviet Union, has a long history of engagement with Africa. The Muscovy and subsequently Russian empires were land based and expanded eastwards from the sixteenth century onwards (Lamb 1948). The only sizeable overseas colony was Alaska, which was sold to the United States in 1867. While Russia did not then have African colonies there was a history of some interaction dating back to the Middle Ages, when Russian and African pilgrims met in the 'Holy Land' (Shubin 2004).

Russian–African relations remained minimal until the period of the Cold War, when the Soviet Union sponsored a variety of libera-tion movements in Africa and subsequently supported independent governments (ibid.). During the Cold War, Africa was a proxy battle-ground for the superpowers and their allies, in addition to being a site of competition between the Soviet Union and China (Meredith 2005).[5] Particularly close relationships were cultivated with certain 'socialist' states such as Angola and Mozambique.

During the Cold War the Soviet Union offered scholarships to African students and a university in Russia was named after Patrice Lumumba, the ill-fated Congolese leader. This has had implications up to the present, as several African leaders were educated in the Soviet Union, including the current Angolan president, who has been in power since 1979, who received his training in petroleum engineering there.

With the end of the Cold War and the collapse of the Soviet Union, Russia turned inwards. This resulted in something of a geopolitical vacuum in Africa, which China, and more recently the United States, among other powers, were to fill (Carmody 2011a). In 1992, for financial reasons, Russia closed three of its African embassies – in Lesotho, Niger and Burkina Faso – and in total a dozen embassies or consulates in Africa were closed down in the post-Cold War era (Shubin 2004). In 1993 a foreign policy document listing Russia's top foreign policy priority regions listed Africa ninth out of ten, one place ahead of Latin America (cited in Fidan and Aras 2010).

Nonetheless, Russia maintained an extensive network of diplomatic representation on the continent, with more than forty embassies. In the 2000s Russia also built the first new embassy complex in Africa for fifteen years, in Ghana, and is set to establish diplomatic relations with the new government of South Sudan. Increased Russian private sector interest in the continent is also evident as illustrated by the Russia-Africa Business Council, founded in 2002.

Arguably Vladimir Putin is a historical *materialist* and realizes that military and political power ultimately flow from economic power. Consequently the economization of relations with Africa was evident from early on in his presidency. In the *Concept of the Foreign Policy of the Russian Federation* in 2000 it was stated that there was a need 'to develop a political dialogue with the Organization of African Unity and with sub-regional organizations' (quoted in Shubin 2004: 105). However, this was connected explicitly to 'their capabilities for enabling Russia to join multilateral economic projects in the continent', where finance would come from outside of Russia, or outside of Africa.

Russian interests in Africa

> Your map of Africa looks nice, but my map of Africa lies in
> Europe. Here is Russia, and here is France, and we are here at the
> very centre; that is my map of Africa. (Otto von Bismarck, quoted
> in Baumgart 1987: 151)

> As to Russia, traditionally with the African continent we've got
> very good relations. We *subtly* feel all the problems of the African
> continent. (Putin 2002, emphasis added)

An academic at the Institute for African Studies in Moscow argues
that the world is 'coming back to "the classical terrain of great power
rivalries" and Africa should be ready to respond to the geopolitical
shifts at work' (Urnov 2009). According to Jordan (2010), the primary
aim of Russian relations with Africa is to increase its influence within
international fora, particularly the G8 (post-)industrial countries.
By gaining new allies Russia could bolster its standing in the G8,
particularly as it was included because of its military, rather than
economic, might, which initially remained the preserve of the G7.
According to Putin's G8 representative in 2003, 'the G8 is a club of
the strong, where you can't come with an outstretched hand, because
you need to pay' (quoted in ibid.: 92).

While Russian trade with Africa is less than a tenth of Chinese
trade, Russia has written off substantially more debt to African countries as it had both given out more loans (during the Soviet era)
and is obliged to engage in debt relief by virtue of its membership
in the G8 (ibid.). Cornelissen (2009) has also argued that Russia
has a particular incentive to accumulate alliance partners from the
global South, including Africa, given encroachment by the USA on its
traditional sphere of influence in eastern Europe and the Caucasus.

Membership of the G8 for Russia, and associated commitments
such as aid and debt relief to Africa, is partly performative – to
show other states in the international system that Russia is a Great
Power. This also serves a domestic political function as it shows the
Russian population that Putin has been successful in the project of
national revival and power projection. In practice, however, Russia
has been a laggard in terms of fulfilling its G8 commitments; but it
is the optics which are politically important. Under the Soviet Union

a well-known adage was 'we'll pretend to work, if you pretend to pay us'. In terms of Russia's initial G8 membership this might have been rephrased to 'We'll pretend you are a Great Power, if you pretend to play with us'.[6] As the G20 is now the primary forum of global economic policy-making, Russia has also arguably played a role in reconfiguring the architecture of global governance to its benefit (Chaturvedi, Fues et al. 2012). However, Russia continues to try to bolster its power through the 'energy superpower' vector.

In common with other members of the BRICS there has been at least a partial economization of Russian relations with Africa, although with some distinctive elements, particularly the attempt to leverage previous relations with old Cold War allies such as Angola. This economization of relations also has a geopolitical dimension, as competition in the international system is now substantially in the realm of economics, rather than security – a new modality of international relations associated with globalization: geopolitical economy.

Russia is pursuing a 'multi-vector' foreign policy and is committed, along with other members of the BRICS, to creating a multipolar world. The basis of Russia's multi-vector policy is based on 'emerging multi-polarity. No one can have a monopoly on globalisation and ever more urgent is the task of providing equal access for all states to its advantages' (Lavrov, quoted in Klomegah 2008). According to one analyst, 'part of the agenda [of Medvedev's 2009 tour of Africa] is to push Russia's credentials as a representative of commodity-rich developing countries with such forums as the G-8 and the G-20' (Weafer, quoted in BBC 2009b).

In the 1960s and 1970s some scholars wrote about the dependence of the Third World on the industrial countries. However, as energy resources have become more in demand and scarce (Klare 2008), with the expansion of the global economy a new type of 'reverse dependence' or interdependence has emerged. While the search for new energy sources has been one of the primary drivers of increased Chinese, Indian and Brazilian engagement in Africa, Russia is the world's biggest energy exporter. The country has more than a third of the world's proven gas reserves and almost 5 per cent of its oil, and in some years exports more oil than Saudi Arabia (Bouzarovksi and

Bassin 2011). Consequently its (re-)engagement with the continent has been much more limited than that of the other members of the BRICS group. For example, Russo-African trade peaked at US$7.3 billion in 2008, a small fraction of China's trade with the continent (African Development Bank 2011). Furthermore, while Russia's imports from Africa have been growing at a compound annual growth rate of 19 per cent for the last decade or so, the continent still accounts for only 1 per cent of Russia's global trade and about 4 per cent of the stock of Russian overseas foreign direct investment (Shubin 2010). Russian companies have around US$4 billion invested in Africa (Urnov 2009).

According to Paul Kennedy (2006), Professor of History at Yale University, Vladimir Putin's interest in meddling in Africa has diminished as there are other more strategic priorities. Nonetheless, Russia has growing economic and geopolitical interests on the continent driven by the linked twin imperatives of the potential exhaustion of its own natural resources (African Development Bank 2011) and its attempts to reassert itself as a Great Power globally (Mankoff 2009). In 2011, at the Russian–African Business Forum in Addis Ababa, Mikhail Margelov, who is a Russian presidential representative, announced that Russia planned to return to Africa in full force (Gabueuv 2011). This is also facilitated by the fact that, in contrast to other members of the BRICS group, because Russia is 'an oil surplus economy [it] has a surplus in general government accounts' (BRICS 2012: 18).

According to former ambassador Urnov (2009), 'Africa and Russia own over 60% of ... world natural resource and their interaction in this field is natural and can be of great benefit to both. The countries whom God blessed with mineral wealth should join forces to save-guard [sic] their sovereign right to control this wealth especially in the face of attempts to declare it "an international asset".' However, given rapid rates of extraction, up to 35 per cent of Russian minerals are losing their commercial profitability. Large Russian natural resource companies consequently need new sources of supply, with Africa a region of great potential in this regard. Furthermore, according to one journalist, 'Russia's own enormous energy resources are located in areas that are not easily accessible, sparsely populated and have extremely unfriendly climatic conditions – so developing them would be a much costlier business than developing the same resources in Africa' (Filavotova 2009). This is echoed by other analysts, who argue that for certain minerals, particularly those to the east of the Ural Mountains, it is sometimes less expensive to extract them from Africa (Urnov 2009).[7] There are thus economic imperatives at play. For Filavatova, however, the primary motive for Russia in attempting to deepen alliances to develop an 'energy rich bloc' is to shift the balance of power in world politics away from the West. Remaining an energy superpower requires access to or otherwise controlling supply. Vladimir Putin has said that the idea of a global gas cartel along the lines of OPEC is an 'interesting one'; a sentiment which is shared by Algerian president Bouteflika (Darbouche 2007). This is difficult, however, as gas is typically sold on long-term contracts tied to the price of oil.

This attempt by Russia to engage in geopolitical balancing, to counter the power of the USA in particular, is useful to African political elites, particularly as Russia has power capabilities such as a permanent seat at the UN Security Council and nuclear weapons, which they do not. Angola is now Africa's second-biggest oil producer, and on the occasion of Russia's national day, President dos Santos of Angola reaffirmed 'the Angolan Government's desire to further strengthen and deepen the historic ties of friendship and mutually beneficial cooperation between the two countries and in defence of their mutual interests'. He also noted with appreciation 'the assumption by Russia of the important role which it plays in the concert of Nations, asserting itself in international relations, as an indispensable factor of balance and guarantee for world peace and security' (Angola Press 2012).

Previously, in 2006, President dos Santos had asked Putin for support in the G8 to help fight pandemics, famine and achieve debt relief in Africa (Jordan 2010). This was arguably somewhat ironic as Dos Santos could have made a substantial contribution to these efforts through his own personal wealth, which is in the hundreds of millions of US dollars. According to Forbes (2011a), his eldest daughter is one of Africa's richest women. She is now Africa's first female billionaire.

Putin has now visited Angola a number of times, and both he and Dos Santos were leading figures in the former 'socialist' regimes in both their countries. Ties between Angola and Russia are formalized through the Angola/Russia Inter-governmental Commission for Economic Cooperation. Russian companies are active there and Alrosa extracts 60 per cent of Angolan diamonds. Angola is the world's fifth-largest diamond producer.

In 2009 the Russian president, Dmitry Medvedev, visited a number of African countries with more than a hundred Russian business people. As part of that trip Mr Medvedev agreed a US$2.5 billion project between Gazprom, the Russian state-owned company, and the Nigerian state oil company to develop gas and oilfields and build a pipeline for gas from Nigeria to Europe. According to a journalist, the Trans-Sahara Gas Pipeline 'would give Russia control over the supply of Nigerian gas to Europe, and thereby reinforce the dependence of European consumers on Russia' (Cohen 2009), although this may be overstating the control which Gazprom would exercise. Russian companies are also active in other sectors in Africa.

Russia is the world's fourteenth-largest foreign investor, with Africa receiving about 9 per cent of that outflow (UNCTAD 2009a). The table below lists some Russian companies' main investment projects on the continent.

While the influence of the state is strong in Russia's relations with Africa, it differs from that of China, for example. While the difference between Chinese state-owned and private companies operating overseas is the difference between being told what to do and being told what not to do (Moyo 2012), and many of the biggest Russian companies engaged on the continent are, in common with China's, state owned, some of the Russian private sector is more autonomous. For example, the investment banking group Renaissance Capital (2013) is very active in Africa, where they have offices in six countries. According to its website, it 'is the leading independent investment bank operating in Russia, the CIS, Central and Eastern Europe, Africa, Asia and other high-opportunity emerging and frontier markets'. It plans to open an office in Rwanda (Ombok 2011). The company's East African headquarters is in Nairobi, where it became 'the third-largest investment bank by value of transactions in Kenya in the first half of this year [2011]' (ibid.). RenCap is half owned by Mikhail Prokhorov, a billionaire political opponent of Vladimir Putin. The company

TABLE 5.1 Selected Russian companies operative in Africa

Country	Company
Algeria	Gazprom: gas exploration; Rosneft: gas exploration
Angola	Alrosa: mining
Botswana	Norilsk Nickel: mining
Burkina Faso	Severstal: steel production
DRC	Arlan Invest Holding: financing of diamond exploration; Alrosa: mining
Egypt	Lukoil: oil production; Rosatom: uranium exploration and mining
Gabon	Renova Group: mining
Ghana	Lukoil: oil
Guinea	Rusal: aluminium production
Ivory Coast	Lukoil: oil
Kenya	Renaissance Capital: financial services
Liberia	Severstal: steel production
Libya	Gazprom: gas exploration; Rosneft: gas
Namibia	Renova Group: mining; Rosatom: mining
Nigeria	Gazprom: oil and gas; Rusal: mining; Rosatom: nuclear energy
South Africa	Renova Group: mining; Norilsk Nickel: mining; Evraz: steel
Sudan	Rosneft: oil exploration; Slavneft: oil exploration

Source: Edinger (n.d.)

is also important in terms of discourse, promoting Africa now as the 'fastest' rather than the 'bottom billion', in terms of economic growth (Robertson 2012).

(Re)constructing Russia in and through Africa

'Since the collapse of Communism, Russia has endured a confusing, often torturous process of self-definition' (Mankoff 2009: 11). Another analyst argues that 'No nation ever poured more intellectual energy into answering the question of national identity than Russia' (Billington 2004: 12). Russia, along with Turkey, straddles both Europe and Asia. This has meant that both countries have a somewhat uneasy relationship with the European Union, for example, as they are considered by many to be a part of Europe and also somewhat separate or distinct from it. The geopolitical upheaval of the collapse of the Soviet Union resulted in a dramatic repositioning of the country from a developed to a 'developing' one, even if the terminology of 'transition economies' was coined in order to avoid this implication (Gray 2011). The economic and political turmoil of the 1990s in Russia laid the ground for the subsequent election of Vladimir Putin.

The Putinist revival of Russian power has had a number of interrelated axes. The revival of the Russian economy, based on high energy export prices, facilitated the rebuilding of the Russian military. Russian companies are once more developing leading-edge military technology (Weir 2010). Additionally Russia has transitioned from being an aid recipient to being both an aid donor and a recipient. According to the World Bank, Russia is now a major donor to low-income countries (Provost 2011). Furthermore, in August 2011 it was announced that Russia would establish an Agency for International Development in 2012 (Gray n.d.), although this had yet to be launched as of 2012 as a result of intergovernmental department turf wars (Oxford Analytica 2012). This could be read as another marker of Russia's return to 'Great Power' status. Russia also allows duty-free imports from least developed countries (Edinger n.d.), and policies such as this also facilitated Russia's entry into the World Trade Organization in 2012, which could have been blocked by any other member.

Africa plays an important symbolic role in this (re)construction of the Russian state imaginary, as 'it is by using Africa as a fulcrum that Russia attempts to lever itself out of the West–East axis as a transitioning recipient country and into the North–South axis as an emerging donor country' (Gray 2011: 8). Despite the fact that the bulk of Russian official development assistance is concentrated, for geo-strategic reasons, in the Newly Independent States of Central Asia in particular, in official pronouncements Africa is given prominence. This is because 'Africa is the arena where they can demonstrate their power and privilege by rendering aid to those presumed to be perpetually powerless and underprivileged' (ibid.: 8). The Russian mass media frequently use Africa as a 'zero baseline', and the continent serves in the popular media imaginary to define Russia through its othering.

Russia has cultivated relations with former client states in Africa, such as Angola, where some former 'socialist' parties have successfully reinvented themselves to stay in power (Ishiyama 2004). In much of post-independence Africa the state has been the primary locus of economic accumulation (Ravenhill 1986), and arguably Russia is now learning from the strategy of political accumulation pioneered by leaders such as Dos Santos in Africa, where political power is used to accumulate personal wealth.[8]

Reportedly President Putin also encouraged and facilitated a joint venture operation (United Manganese of Kalahari) between the Russian Renova group and a front company of South Africa's ruling ANC to prospect in the North Cape region of that country, which is thought to hold 80 per cent of the world's commercially exploitable manganese (Pham 2008). The Soviet Union supported the ANC during its liberation struggle.

In common with China, Russia is arguably a status quo power in Africa. In reference to the 'Arab Spring', the Russian foreign minister (Lavrov 2012) argues that:

> We are well aware of the fact that the transformation of a society is a complex and generally long process which rarely goes smoothly … Russia probably knows the true cost of revolutions better than most other countries. We are fully aware that revolutionary changes are always accompanied by social and economic setbacks as well as by loss of human life and suffering. This is exactly why we support an evolutionary and peaceful way of enacting long-awaited changes in the Middle East and North Africa … There are many indications that things are far from being good in Libya after the ousting of Muammar Gaddafi. Instability has spread further to the Sahara and Sahel region, and the situation in Mali was dramatically aggravated.

There is undoubtedly merit in this argument. Revolutions do tend to result in substantial loss of life, and Lavrov does note that he and the Russian Federation support the people of the Arab world in their struggles for freedom and prosperity. However, what does the Russian position translate to in practice? Russia, along with China, is very concerned about protecting its domestic sovereignty and sphere of influence in its 'near abroad'. In general, this has translated into support for incumbent regimes against pressure for 'regime change'. Arms exports to repressive regimes, such as Sudan, must be read in that light. Globalization is meant to result in a permeability or even elimination of borders, but national sovereignty is still a powerful ideational construct and Russia is one of its primary defenders.

Authoritarian aid and arms to Africa?

Recently in Western policy, media and academic circles there has been substantial concern about the growing geopolitical roles of China and Russia and the way in which they spread their influence in the developing world. One of the vectors through which this influence is meant to be developed is through 'authoritarian aid' (Radio Free Europe and Radio Liberty 2009), whereby authoritarian (China) or 'soft authoritarian' (Russia) states give financial support to 'rogue states' in the developing world. Both Russia and China have supplied the Sudanese government with weaponry, including advanced attack helicopters in the Russian case, which have been used to deadly effect against civilian populations. During the conflict in Darfur in the early 2000s some of the Antonov bombers were being flown by Russian pilots (Jok 2007). As noted earlier, however, a detailed analysis found that the USA was more likely to export weapons to dictatorships in Africa than China (Midford and Soysa 2012). Nonetheless, Russia has played a leading role in arms exports to Africa.

Russia is the world's second-largest arms exporter after the United States, and while the total varied from year to year, during the period 2005–09 14 per cent of its arms and weapons exports went to Africa, which was its second-largest market (study undertaken by Africa Europe Faith and Justice Network 2010). Arms exports are one area where Russia has retained a competitive advantage in manufacturing in the post-Cold War era, given the extent of investment during the Soviet era and high cost and technological barriers to entry (Chossudovsky 2002). In 2011, over 9 per cent of Russia's arms exports went to Africa (calculated from Stockholm International Peace Research Institute 2012). The military equipment of some former socialist regimes such as Angola and Ethiopia is 90 per cent of Soviet origin according to some estimates (Fidan and Aras 2010).

TABLE 5.2 Russian arms exports to Africa (US$ millions)

	2010	2011	Total
Algeria	698	663	1,361
Chad	7		7
Egypt	340	300	640
Ethiopia	54		54
Guinea		1	1
Kenya	20		20
Libya	15		15
South Sudan		61	61
Sudan	41	63	104
Uganda		237	237
Total			2,499

Source: Stockholm International Peace Research Institute (2012)

However, paradoxically, Russia, along with the world's other biggest arms exporters, has been active in peacekeeping efforts in Africa, at the same time as being a major arms supplier. For example, in the early 2000s Russia sent 115 military personnel and four MI-24 attack helicopters to Sierra Leone in support of the peacekeeping process in that country (Vassiliev 2003, cited in Shubin 2004).

While total Russian arms exports to Africa totalled 'only' US$1.4 billion from 1999 to 2006, on President Putin's visit to Algeria in 2006, arms purchases totalling US$7.5 billion were announced in exchange for the cancellation of Algeria's debt to Russia of US$4.7 billion (Fidan and Aras 2010; Edinger n.d.). As a result of this arms deal, over the next few years 'Algeria stood to receive over 600 combat aircraft, 22 bomber aircraft, 8 air defence systems, 2 submarines, tanks, 2 naval guns, over 4000 missiles, and other arms from the Russian state arms exporter Rosoboronexport as part of a modernizing overhaul of Algeria's military capacity' (study undertaken by Africa Europe Faith and Justice Network 2010: 37–8). This represents a transformation of the Algerian state's military capability, and high-tech military exports may presage an alternative future in Russo-African relations, according to some analysts.

The 'multi-vector' nature of Russia's foreign policy was in evidence during Putin's 2006 trip as he reportedly also attempted to broker a deal which would allow for debt relief in exchange for investment in the 'untouchable' Algerian state-owned gas company Sonatrach, but this was not achieved, as the Algerians prize their autonomy (Finon 2007). This would have been geopolitically attractive because between them Gazprom and Sonatrach supply 40 per cent of the European Union's gas. Nonetheless, European officials have expressed concerns about the Memorandum of Understanding which was signed between the two companies (Darbouche 2007), although this proved to be unfounded (Finon 2007), as supply disruption also hurts the Russian economy.

Reflecting on the mirror

The Putinist reconstruction of Russia, then, contains both representational and material dimensions, which interact. The reassertion of Russia as a Great Power requires both cooperation and competition with 'the West' (particularly the United States) and the construction of new alliances, through the BRICS cooperation mechanism, for example, in addition to cooperation through overseas development assistance.[9] In Africa, cooperation between the West and Russia is manifest in coordinated naval patrols with NATO ships off the coast of Somalia.

Both Russia and China are pursuing statist models of globalization, although these are somewhat different in content. In the Chinese case state-owned corporations are in the lead, whereas in the Russian case both large-scale private and state-owned corporations have been undertaking substantial investments overseas. Paradoxically, in the Russian case the growth of state-connected corporate capital has been facilitated by some highly neoliberal policies, particularly the fact that Russia is a low 'flat tax' state (Peck 2004) – a hybrid neoliberal/statist regime.

Overall, Africa remains somewhat marginal to Russian foreign policy concerns, although it has taken a more active interest in the continent in the last decade in particular, for the reasons mapped out in this chapter. Economically Africa is important as a site of expansion for Russian natural resource companies and a market for arms exports. However, as Russia does not produce the types of low-cost manufactures that China does, which have a ready market in Africa, and is also natural resource rich, its relations with the continent are likely to remain more muted than those of the other BRICS powers. Indeed, according to a Russian diplomat working in Africa, 'It is useless to fight with the Chinese. They give Africa colossal amounts of credit on very good terms' (quoted in Gabueuv 2011). However, as a (re-)emerging Great Power Russia takes an active foreign policy interest in all world regions. It does not have the material (economic and military) capabilities of either the United States or increasingly China, and consequently it is attempting to leverage old Cold War relations to increase its power in Africa.

Russian foreign policy is still formulated primarily in relation and opposition to the United States (Mankoff 2009). For example, Russia offered Kyrgyzstan US$2 billion after it said it would close its American military base (Economist 2009). Various incidents and confrontations between Russia and the USA led Republican presidential candidate Mitt Romney to label Russia America's 'number one geopolitical foe' (Johnson 2012). Russian political elites arguably enjoy such rhetoric as it confirms for them the resurgence of Russia as a Great Power (Mankoff 2009), and President Putin even thanked Romney for stating his position so clearly. Russian relations with Africa should be viewed primarily through this geopolitical code; as a site where Russia competes with the United States. This representational politics and the metageographies (which people carry in their heads) are important because it is by reference to the post-Soviet failures of the past and Russia's current revival as a Great Power that Putin is able to legitimize his continued hold on power domestically. Thus the materiality of Russian re-engagement in Africa is, for the moment at least, arguably of secondary importance to its ideational meaning and impacts.

6 | BRAZIL: GLOBALIZING SOLIDARITY OR LEGITIMIZING ACCUMULATION?

Brazil's impressive social gains have become the envy of the developing world, turning Brazil into a laboratory and model for globalisation with a social conscience. (Sweig 2010)

Africa's natural resources and potential markets have made the continent a priority area for Brazil. Facilitated and supported by political and diplomatic initiatives, spearheaded by giant resources companies, underpinned by infrastructure enterprises, and assisted by cultural affinities, Brazil, like its fellow industrialised developing world giants, China and India, is returning to Africa in a big way. (Campbell 2007)

Brazil's intensified engagement with Africa demonstrates both geopolitical ambition and economic interest, but its strong historical ties and affinities with Africa set it apart from the other original BRIC countries. (World Bank and IPEA 2011: 3)

In 2012 Brazil overtook the United Kingdom to become the world's sixth-largest economy, and it is thought that it will soon overtake France to become the fifth largest. This represents a very significant shift in the global geo-economic order, as two of the foremost Great Powers of the previous three centuries are supplanted in (economic) importance by a former Portuguese colony from 'the other West'. Per capita incomes in Brazil, of course, remain much lower, at around a third of those of the United Kingdom, but the country can arguably now claim to be a 'Great Power', even if this is not reflected, yet, in current global governance arrangements, through a permanent seat on the United Nations Security Council, for example, and Brazil still has a lower voting share in the IMF than Belgium (McCulloch and Sumner 2009). Nonetheless, Brazil's drive to 'Great Power' status is reflected in its development of its own nuclear submarine programme, for example (Daily Mail 2011); although these subs will be nuclear propelled rather than armed.

As a reflection of both its growing economy and geopolitical influence the Brazilian footprint has expanded dramatically in Africa in the last decade. However, as the opening quotes to the chapter intimate, the nature of Brazilian engagement with the continent has been distinctive for reasons of both history and economic structure and class. What is the nature of Brazilian engagement in Africa? Is it cooperative, exploitative or a combination of the two, and how have domestic politics informed this? In order to understand the nature of Afro-Brazilian relations it is first necessary to place them in the context of the country's foreign policy more broadly, and then examine the specificities of the relationship.

Global Brazil and Africa

Some have argued that after the Cold War Brazil attempted to create a 'consensual hegemony' in South America, whereby other countries were recruited to achieve Brazilian goals, without the threat of force (Burges 2008). Greater regional influence would in turn, it was felt, facilitate greater global influence for Brazil.

In the mid-1990s one of the world's foremost dependency theorists, Fernando Henrique Cardoso, was elected president of Brazil. While many on the left pilloried him for his conservative macroeconomic management, his presidency was still informed by his (previous) ideology. However, he felt that the rapid evolution and diffusion of technology in particular had changed the context of economic development and argued that while globalization would provide a 'shock' to the Brazilian economy, it could be turned to national economic and political advantage through the embedding of democracy and through appropriate policies over the medium term.

The deepening of Brazil's engagement with the international system under Cardoso's premiership and the emergent commodity 'super-cycle', led by demand for natural resources from China in particular from the early 2000s, sparked a major revival of the Brazilian economy. This was also facilitated by the fact that as a result of previous import-substitution policies, Brazil had a number of substantial, competitive and in some cases technologically advanced businesses, such as the aerospace company Embraer. An old aphorism is that 'Brazil is the country of the future ... and always will be'. However, this is no longer the case as an economically revived 'global Brazil' increasingly extends worldwide influence.

The election of Lula da Silva as Brazilian president in 2002 marked another significant shift in that country's politics which was reflected both in domestic social policy and in international relations. There are a number of tenets which guide Brazilian foreign policy: multilateralism, regional integration and South–South cooperation. Indeed, according to the Brazilian constitution, in its international relations it is governed by the principles of 'cooperation among people for the progress of humanity' (quoted in Saravia 2012: 117). These guiding principles are aimed at achieving a multipolar world order favourable to increasing Brazilian influence and domestic poverty reduction.

In terms of Africa, White (2010: 222) explores three vectors or axes of Brazilian engagement, which 'exudes an increasing sense of responsibility along with a strategic impetus'. These are political diplomacy, development cooperation and 'African neo-mercantilism', or Brazilian exploitation of opportunities for trade and investment. Development cooperation facilitates both alliance building and commercial penetration, and Brazil now has an Overseas Development Assistance Programme, more than half of which is directed to Africa. The Department for Africa and the Middle East was also broken up and the dedicated Division for Africa reactivated in the Foreign Ministry (Oliveira Ribeiro 2009).

Along the neo-mercantilist vector, Brazil also has major corporations, such as one of the world's biggest natural resource companies, Vale, engaged in major projects in Africa. While Lula indicated that he wished to change the structure of Brazil's export basket and move it away from primary commodities towards high-value-added manufactured goods, this has not, in general, occurred.[1] However, Brazilian exports to Africa are heavily concentrated in manufacturing and are rising rapidly. Consequently Africa is an increasingly important market for Brazilian goods as it attempts to diversify both the structure and geography of its trade. Africa now accounts for about a twentieth of Brazilian exports; more than France and Germany combined (Tavener 2012). Consequently the continent is an important market, and also aid destination and source of raw materials, for Brazil. Brazilian relations with Africa exhibit elements of both co-operative and competitive globalization (Nederveen Pieterse 2010).

According to White (2010: 229), Brazil seems to have adopted a middle path between the Chinese and Indian approaches to engagement with Africa. The Chinese approach to engagement is highly political and supported through the state-driven investments and development initiatives, while the Indian approach is more private sector led. However, the Brazilian approach to Africa is not only based around strategic choices about what will be most effective in furthering the country's interests, but also a vision of global cooperation driven by domestic class politics, whereby the majority see the need to reduce massive domestic inequality. This is the tension in Brazilian relations with Africa – the overseas expansion of resource conglomerates, which facilitate economic growth domestically and create resources for redistribution, is involved in displacement and inequality generation in Africa. The Brazilian state attempts to square the circle, and also facilitate market access for its corporations, through its overseas assistance programme, but the contradictions of this modality of geopolitics remain.

This chapter examines ways in which elements of Brazil's domestic class compromise have informed, and to some extent have been externalized in, its relations with Africa. According to Marques and Mendes (2006), Lula felt he could represent the different social classes of Brazil. During the 2000s it was exporters who created most of the economic growth in the country and 'the boom in exports under Lula combined with the president's aggressive sponsorship of trade missions to Asia, Africa and the Middle East' (Cason and Power 2009: 129) allowed Brazilian business and worker interests to largely coincide. This represents a 'spatial fix' (Harvey 1982) to the contradiction between capital and labour in Brazil, but the imperatives of accumulation and (overseas) legitimization have also been extended to Africa and elsewhere, as detailed below.

There are also geopolitical dimensions to Brazil's strategy, as it engages in alliance-building in Africa to enable 'soft balancing' of US power in the global political economy. According to Burges (2009: 1), rather than overt intervention being the norm, Brazil's strategy has been to hide the country's aspirations to hemispheric and global leadership behind technocratic apolitical programmes, wrapped in a discourse of multilateralism. One of the main innovations under Cardoso's presidency was the introduction of dependency theory into Brazilian foreign policy, in an attempt to reorient global and other scales of relations in order to advance Brazilian development. Brazilian 'consensual hegemony' is aimed at allowing the country to lead through 'soft power', despite a deficiency of other power resources (ibid.).

Geopolitics also feeds into geo-economics as Lula sought to reshape international economic geography by increasing the importance of South–South flow, but in an explicitly liberal way (Burges 2007: 1354). This was underpinned by Lula's doctrine of '*auto-estima*' or self-confidence, the belief that countries of the global South could influence the nature of global economic and political structures (Burges 2009). Whereas the earlier round of globalization associated with the offshoring of manufacturing investment from the global North to the global South created a 'new international division of labour' (Frobel et al. 1980), Brazil under Lula sought to create a newer international division of labour centred on South–South flows. This type of 'economic entangling' (Paul 2005) is aimed at shifting 'relative economic power through trading blocs and other types of sector cooperation that increase the economic growth of members while directing trade away from non-members' (Flemes 2009: 166). Thus it has a geopolitical objective, and also allows further revision of global governance to allow for the creation of rules more favourable to development in (parts of) the global South – a virtuous circle of geopolitical economy.

This chapter reflects on Africa's positionality in Brazilian foreign policy and the ways in which this has facilitated alliance-building in fora such as the World Trade Organization, where African countries have supported Brazilian positions, sometimes seemingly in opposition to their own (immediate) material interests. While Nigel Harris (1986) announced 'the end of the Third World' twenty years ago, based on differential economic performance, current patterns of globalization and increasing South–South interaction have given both increased structure and power to these (re-)emerging alliances.[2]

This chapter also reviews the nature of current Brazilian political and economic engagements with Africa, but differs from others in trying to assess the theoretical significance of these. It seeks to unpack the discursive construction of emergent 'South Space' – the idea of the global South as a homogenized post-colonial region with similar interests, in the face of continued uneven development and the differential construction of Brazilian-centred and inflected trans-localities in Africa. The relationship between 'South Space horizontal cooperation' and differentiated and hierarchically organized pro-cesses of translocalization is explored. However, in order to explore the present nature of Brazilian engagement, influence and impact on Africa it is necessary to situate the relationship historically in order to understand how this influences current geopolitical relations.

The geopolitics of Afro-Brazilian relations

There has been a long history of engagement between Africa and Brazil, largely arising from the transatlantic slave trade. In contrast to popular assumptions in some countries, most slaves who were kidnapped from Africa went to Latin America and the Caribbean, rather than North America. British North America and the USA are estimated to have only received 4.4 per cent of the total, as against 35 per cent for Brazil by itself (Thomas 1997; Lovejoy 2000, in Lineback and Lineback Gritzner 2010). In some cases there were also instances of 'reverse migration'. The Tabom community in Ghana is descended from 'returned' Brazilian slaves.

Since the 1960s, at least some members of the Brazilian military and political elite have sought to make Brazil a 'Great Power'. This thinking may have been partly inspired by *Mundonovismo* or 'New Worldism' in the early part of the twentieth century, which envisaged the decline of Europe and Latin American prominence (Captain 2010). After the banning of the slave trade relations became more muted, until the 1960s – the era of African independence.

Despite his social democratic credentials Lula de Silva also sought to make Brazil a Great Power, while not using this language. Another way to view this is as an attempt to ward off weakness and vulner-ability to external interference. In relation to Africa, this has meant that Brazil has rediscovered its 'Atlantic vocation', framed within a broader context of formulating more effective responses to the challenges posed by globalization (Alden 2009: 17). This also has a military dimension to it.

Brazil is, for example, developing its own nuclear submarine programme, in part to protect its trade and newly discovered oil reserves in the South Atlantic. The re-creation of the US 4th Fleet in the South Atlantic may also have inspired this (Visentini 2010). While there may be some civilian and commercial spin-offs from this programme, and Brazil has been relatively successful in developing high-tech industries such as computing and aerospace (Schmitz and Hewitt 1991), the primary goals of this programme are security and prestige related. Having its own nuclear submarine programme is what a 'Great' or even middle power 'should do' (Wendt 1999). South Africa has also bought high-tech submarines and Brazil and South Africa have a military alliance called Atlasur, along with Argentina and Uruguay, which allows for training exercises and information and technology sharing on naval affairs (Doelling 2008).

Lula also said that Brazil has the largest African population of any country after Nigeria and that consequently the continent was a cradle of Brazilian civilization. In 2010 over half of Brazil's population were of African descent (World Bank and IPEA 2011). While acknowledging that South America was Brazil's foreign policy priority, Lula said in relation to Africa that 'we are committed to share the destiny and challenges of the region' (quoted in White 2010: 229). Indeed, some Brazilian diplomats went farther and argued that Africa could be considered the eastern part of Brazil (Captain 2010). In Brazil there is a doctrine of 'living borders' whereby they are zones of cooperation rather than separation (Burges 2009). This has fed into discourse about Africa being Brazil's 'eastern frontier', for example. 'These proximity arguments seek to guarantee Brazil a privileged status in Africa and represent a normative justification for geopolitical interests' (Barbosa et al. 2009: 72). Brazilian diplomats are aware that the country cannot compete with established Great Powers (Flemes 2009); hence the imperative of 'soft power' projection, of which 'blackness' represents one dimension. While the deep historical connections between Brazil and Africa can be used for strategic gain they are also no doubt also genuinely felt, and this common feeling and empathy are among the strategic 'soft power' advantages that Brazilian actors bring to their engagement with the continent.

There are also linkages forged from more recent historical interactions. While relations were in abeyance after the suppression of the slave trade, during the era of the Brazilian military dictatorship, from 1964 to 1985, a doctrine of 'Responsible Pragmatism' was adopted. This suggested that Brazil should diversify its international relations to decrease dependence on the United States. A number of resource-for-manufactures swaps were also struck with post-independence African countries, making Brazil an important source of imports for a time. Brazil was also the first country to recognize independent Angola and offered support through construction projects and other investments (White 2010). The Brazilian private construction conglomerate Odebrecht first invested there in 1982, while Petrobras, which is widely held to be the largest company headquartered in the southern hemisphere,[3] first invested there in 1979 and has operations in more than a dozen African countries. This Brazilian 'first mover' advantage is still evident in Angola, for example, through Brazilian television and brands,[4] and there are over a hundred Brazilian companies active in the country (Seibert 2012). It was the deployment of Brazilian peacekeepers there under the auspices of the UN in the early 2000s after the civil war had ended which reanimated Brazilian companies' interest in the country (Vigevani and Cepaluni 2009).

On coming to power Lula sought to further alter the global balance of power (Greider and Rapoza 2003) and made Africa a priority. He sought to leverage historical relations between Brazil and the continent and was particularly active in Africa during his term. He repeatedly said that the twenty-first century would be Africa and Latin America's (Captain 2010) and signed 112 treaties with thirty-seven African countries (Doelling 2008). In recognition of his commitment to the continent, in 2009 he was the guest of honour at the African Union summit. In common with the other BRICS powers, Brazil under Lula pursued and continues to pursue a multi-vector foreign policy in Africa. The template which is being followed is the same as that which has been applied in South America.

In the South American case Brazil looks to 'create economic opportunities for itself, which might offer opportunities to regional "partners". The goal is to make South America a vibrant market for Brazilian products and a source for the energy resources that the country's economy needs. This pragmatic and self-serving market-friendly attitude is not neoliberal at its core – it deploys the state in support of national firms exploiting regional and global opportunities' (Burges 2007: 1344). According to Burges, this is a neostructuralist approach whereby the state does not attempt to bring about economic development directly, but clears barriers of either market failure or excessive interventionism to private sector development.

There have, however, been setbacks to Brazilian 'consensual hegemony' in South America, such as the partial nationalization of Bolivia's gas fields operated by Petrobras. This has given added impetus to seeking out new sources of natural resource supply, such as natural gas from Nigeria (Oliveira Ribeiro 2009) and growth for Brazilian transnationals in Africa, with property protection offered by bilateral investment treaties, which often have stronger investment protections than multilateral treaties.[5] Thus there is no neat separation between Brazilian geopolitics and economics in Africa.

According to Paul (2005), sovereignty will increasingly be defined not by the ability to shelter from external influences, but the ability to engage effectively in international institutions. This is reflected in the Brazilian foreign policy doctrines of autonomy through engagement with the global system and diversification of relationships with different partners (Vigevani and Cepaluni 2009). A strategic coupling with Africa results from the fact that 'the new Africa coincides with a global Brazil' (World Bank and IPEA 2011: 3) and these new connections are physically manifest through the construction of a fibre-optic cable linking Brazil to Africa, which is expected to be completed in 2013, and direct flights from Luanda to Brazil are booked months in advance, as many Angolan tourists travel there. The overall goal is global multipolarization (Flemes 2009).

In contrast to Russia's emphasis on renewed hard power, Brazil has a 'soft balancing' strategy whereby it builds alliances to engage with and thereby reduce the power of the United States. 'Soft balancing does not directly challenge US military preponderance, but rather uses non-military tools to delay, frustrate, and undermine the superpowers' unilateral policies' (ibid.: 165). As part of its effort to rebalance 'asymmetric globalisation' (Cardoso, quoted in Bowles 2002), new institutions, such as the India, Brazil, South Africa (IBSA) forum (2003) were created, largely at Brazilian instigation, although it also fitted with the South African government's declared 'butterfly strategy' to forge stronger South–South links with Asia and Latin America.

This alliance was convened primarily, in the first instance, to lobby around issues of interest in the World Trade Organization (Smith 2012). The constitution of IBSA was interesting as all three countries were democracies. This spoke to the bargaining function of this alliance as it sought to influence Western countries in particular on issues like agricultural subsidies. However, the growing economic power of the BRICS group perhaps means that this is of less importance and IBSA has now been largely superseded by the BRICS coordination mechanism.

Other new institutions such as the Africa–South America Cooperation Forum were also initiated to facilitate cooperation in fields such as energy (Africa–South America Cooperation Forum 2006), and the power of Brazil in existing international organizations was also increased through this and its growing economic weight, as evidenced by the election of a Brazilian to lead the United Nations Food and Agriculture Organization (World Bank and IPEA 2011). Furthermore, deepening economic engagement is complemented by deepening political engagement and aid flows.

Brazil has other substantial 'soft power' advantages in Africa by virtue of its success in poverty reduction and the effective way in which it dealt with the HIV/AIDS epidemic (Okumu 2002). Already by 2008 Brazil had halved the percentage of people living below the internationally defined absolute poverty level of a dollar a day; seven years ahead of the Millennium Development Goal target (Constantine, in Mawdsley 2012).[6] Brazil has a highly regarded 'zero hunger' programme which is being replicated in other developing countries. Also, Brazilian companies tend to hire more local staff, which increases their attraction to governments (World Bank and IPEA 2011).

Brazilian economic engagements with Africa

During his tenure, with diplomatic and commercial interests in mind, Lula stayed silent on crises such as those in Darfur and

Zimbabwe (Sweig 2010). This was perhaps not so much to do with direct ties to those countries, but with the broader engagement with Africa, where criticism by leaders of other incumbent regimes has also been muted. Nonetheless, 'joint projects are under way in Sudan and Zimbabwe, where Brazilian ethanol plants have been installed' (World Bank and IPEA 2011: 71).

Quite a lot has now been written about Brazilian economic engagement with Africa as its scale has increased dramatically in the past decade. This is part of a broader trend of growing trade and investment in Africa. While instability in North Africa resulted in a reduction in overall global inward FDI to the continent in recent years, inward investment to SSA increased from $29 billion in 2010 to $37 billion in 2011 (UNCTAD 2012). In 2006 Brazil sent more investment overseas than it received, for the first time ever (Barbosa et al. 2009). Brazilian FDI into Africa has been growing rapidly as part of this general trend, and some estimates suggest that Brazilian companies have hundreds of billions of dollars invested in Africa; although these include investments that may have been routed through offshore tax havens (World Bank and IPEA 2011).

According to the World Bank and IPEA (ibid.), South Africa and Angola were the two biggest recipients of Brazilian FDI on the continent, with Angola receiving US$124 million worth in 2009. However, it should also be remembered that 'South African' companies such as Anglo-American are also substantial investors in Brazil, where they have invested more than Brazilian companies have in South Africa (White 2010). Information on recent or ongoing programmes is not readily available, which may well be linked to the recorded drop in outward FDI, associated with the desire to protect and bolster indigenous industries in the wake of the global financial crisis. Brazilian investment in Africa is concentrated in infrastructure, energy and mining.

The largest Brazilian firms operating in Africa in terms of investment are:

- Andrade Gutierrez, which is a large conglomerate involved in construction, concessions in public utilities and services and telecommunications.

TABLE 6.1 Selected Brazilian enterprises in Africa by name, industry and destination country

Adeco Agropecuária	Sugar and ethanol	Mozambique
Andrade Gutierrez	Construction	Algeria, Angola, Cameroon, Equatorial Guinea, Libya, Mauritania and Republic of the Congo
Aquamec Equipamentos Ltd	Water treatment	Angola
Camargo Corrêa	Construction	Angola, Morocco, Mozambique and South Africa
Vale	Mining and metals	Angola, Guinea, Mozambique and South Africa
Marcopolo S.A.	Bus manufacture	Egypt (joint venture with a national enterprise, GB Auto S.A.E.) and South Africa
Medabil	Construction materials	Angola
Odebrecht	Diversified, but mainly construction	Angola, Botswana, Djibouti, Gabon, Liberia, Libya, Mozambique, Republic of the Congo and South Africa
Symnetics Management	Consultancy	Angola
Volkswagen Caminhões	Minibus manufacture	South Africa
Weg S.A.	Electromechanical	Algeria, Angola, Botswana, Cameroon, Côte d'Ivoire, Democratic Republic of the Congo, Ghana, Guinea, Kenya, Mauritania, Morocco, Mozambique, Namibia, Niger, Nigeria, South Africa, Togo, Tunisia, Zambia and Zimbabwe

Source: Barbosa et al. (2009)

- Camargo Corrêa, which is engaged in construction, real estate, cement production, shipbuilding and footwear production, among other sectors. The company already has investments of US$8 billion on the continent, largely in cement production in Mozambique and Angola (Selvanayagam 2011).
- Odebrecht is involved in construction, water supply and waste treatment, energy production, transportation and logistics, environmental engineering, defence, and sugar production. It is very heavily involved in Angola and reportedly has its own passport line for its employees when they enter the country. The company is the largest private sector employer in Angola; a testament to both the scale of its operation and the extent to which some Brazilian companies hire local workers. The company employs 30,000 people in Angola (Martins n.d.).
- Petrobras, noted earlier, forecast that it would make an investment of $3 billion in Africa between 2011 and 2013, mostly in Angola and Nigeria (Lewis 2011a).
- Queiroz Galvão, a corporation engaged in construction, oil and gas, steel production, food, and public concessions.
- Vale, a major mining, metals and logistics company, is reportedly the second-largest natural resource company worldwide, and its African operations have been highly controversial. It announced in December 2011 that it intends to invest US$1.95 billion in Africa in the coming year (Campbell 2011). Vale has said it will invest a total of between $15 and 20 billion in Africa during the next five years – mostly in Mozambique, Zambia, Guinea and Liberia (Lewis 2011a). Currently, Vale estimates its investments in Africa at $7.7 billion (Bonilla 2012).

There is also growing Brazilian FPI into Africa. In 2012, Brazil's biggest investment bank – BTG Pactual – released plans for a US$1 billion investment fund for Africa (Kinch 2012). Imports from Africa now constitute about a tenth of Brazil's total, whereas exports from Brazil to Africa account for about a twentieth of the total (White 2010). Much of this imported material is oil, with Nigeria accounting for about a third of total African exports to Brazil.

The fact that Brazilian companies hire more local workers

compared to their Chinese counterparts, which often receive con-
cessional state financing, is one way in which Brazilian firms win
contracts in Africa. For example, in Odebrecht's reconstruction of
the Liberian railway system they opted to hire local people from
communities along the railway, rather than import heavy machinery
to do much of the work (Lewis 2011a). "'It worked perfectly well,"
says project manager Pedro Paulo Tosca, who decided to divide the
240km (149 miles) of track into sections and assign dozens of separate
villages along the way to clear them. "The majority of the heavy
work ... was activities that we could perform with local manpower
instead of bringing sophisticated equipment to the site"' (ibid.: 2).

There are also a substantial number of small and medium-sized
(SME) Brazilian enterprises engaged in Africa, involved in sectors
such as food and beverages, automotive parts, clothing and footwear, cosmetics, electronics, housing and construction (World Bank
and IPEA 2011). SMEs have partly engaged in Africa by meeting and
negotiating with African companies at fairs organized by APEX (the
Brazilian Trade and Investment Promotion Agency). For example, at
the APEX fair in São Paulo in 2010, reportedly deals between Brazilian
SMEs and African companies were struck amounting to US$25 million.
Angola has the greatest number of Brazilian SMEs on the continent
and APEX and the Angolan National Purchasing Office cooperate
in a programme to bring basic consumer goods to the population.

The Brazilian National Development Bank (BNDES) is currently the
most popular channel through which to obtain financing for Brazilian
firms investing in Africa. Currently, the BNDES, which is the largest
Latin American bank by assets (Lewis 2011a), has approximately $2 bil-
lion invested in projects on the continent, and it has funded over
thirty infrastructure and ethanol projects by Brazilian companies
in Africa (White 2010). While this figure is small in comparison to
Chinese investment on the continent, and some suggest that Brazil's
investment is limited by its companies' reluctance to invest in what
are perceived to be unstable African economies, BNDES continues
to be very active on the continent. For example, in 2012 BNDES and
the Brazilian bank Bradesco agreed a contract to finance the export
of Brazilian goods for sale in Africa. These exports include industrial
machinery and tools, agricultural machinery and equipment, road

machinery, buses and trucks, generators, transformers and telecommunications equipment made in Brazil (BNDES 2012).

Some have argued that biofuels are a particular axis of engagement from Brazil to Africa, with a senior official at the Brazilian foreign ministry saying the continent was the new biofuels frontier (Barbosa et al. 2009). While Brazil gets more than 80 per cent of its energy requirements from hydroelectric power (World Bank, cited in Government of Brazil 2013), it has a long history of biofuel production, and recent interest and mandated targets in the developed world for biofuel production and consumption, ostensibly to reduce greenhouse gas emissions, have given impetus to this. Investment in oil and biofuel production allowed Brazil to become self-sufficient in energy in 2006 (World Bank and IPEA 2011).

In 2007 Brazil was the largest exporter of ethanol in the world, and it is an area where Brazilian firms have established competitive advantages. Biofuels are one of the key sectors targeted under Brazil's Productive Development Policy (PDP) announced in 2008 and administered by BNDES (Business News Americas 2008). This programme aims to reverse declining competitiveness and make Brazilian firms among the top five in their respective fields, and has a budget of US$125 billion. Manufacturing declined as a share of GDP under the first Lula administration (Prates and Paulani 2007), and was the same in 2011 as in 2007 at around 15 per cent of GDP (World Bank 2012). As part of the PDP there is a Programme of Integration with Africa, which supports Brazilian exports to Africa and disbursed US$360 million in 2009 (World Bank and IPEA 2011). Under this programme a small number of corporations capable of engaging in Africa, usually three, are supported in the different targeted sectors. In Africa some biofuel projects take the form of joint ventures, such as one involving Odebrecht, Sonangol and the Angolan firm Demer (ibid.). However, in Brazil the production of biofuels has sometimes been associated with the use of slave labour (McGrath 2013) and some of these projects have been controversial in Africa.

The veiling of Vale?

Brazilian companies often cooperate with each other. In energy, for example, the two biggest to have led the drive into Africa, Vale and Petrobras, signed a Memorandum of Understanding on potential gas exploration and power generation in Mozambique. Odebrecht uses the Brazilian subsidiary OLEx to support and deliver supplies to its overseas projects, such as those in Angola (Martins n.d.), where the company has over forty projects – more than anywhere else in the world, partly because BNDES has a dedicated US$1.75 billion credit line to support Brazilian companies' projects in Angola (Barbosa et al. 2009). One of these is building the Nosso Super chain of supermarkets in that country. OLEx also sources supplies for these, such as tilapia fish from the Mixed Cooperative of Southern Lowlands Shellfish Gatherers in Brazil, which is supported by the Odebrecht Foundation. In Moatize in Mozambique, Vale relied on twenty other Brazilian companies to build its mega-mine there (Visentini 2010).

Vale is the world's second-largest natural resource company, after BHPBilliton. It is one of the twenty-five largest publicly listed and privately traded companies in the world, and its shares were worth US$176 billion in 2011, having risen more than twenty-five times since it was first listed in 1997 (Geromel 2011). The particularly close relationship between the Brazilian state and Vale is partly explained by the fact that roughly a quarter of the company's shares are indirectly owned by government-run companies, such as Previ, which is the pension fund for employees of the state-owned Banco do Brasil. Through their voting rights these companies exercise substantial control over the make-up of the Vale board.

After leaving office Lula said that he wanted to maintain a role in Africa, which he has done, although not perhaps in the way some might envisage. While he has been appointed to represent Brazil at the African Union, in 2011 Lula also visited Guinea to launch a major Vale project in that country (ibid.).

According to the former president of the company, Africa was 'the next horizon in the industry of natural resources in the world' and 'the future of Vale' (quoted in White 2010: 231). The company has been involved in Africa since 2004, and in 2010 it said it would be investing between US$15 and 20 billion on the continent in the coming five years, with more than US$2.5 billion having already been invested (World Bank and IPEA 2011). In a remarkably short space of time Vale's 'regionality index' has risen to over 20 per cent for Africa, which is substantially higher than for other Brazilian TNCs operative on the continent (Fundação Dom Cabral and the Columbia Programme on International Investment 2007, cited in Barbosa et al. 2009).[7] It is important to remember, however, that only six out of the top twenty Brazilian transnationals have substantial operations in Africa.

In 2012, after a public vote, Vale won the Public Eye award – also known as the 'Nobel Prize of Shame' – for being the worst corporation in the world (Amazon Watch, International Rivers 2012). In 2011 it generated US$22 billion in profits, from revenues of almost US$62 billion (International Movement of People Affected by Vale 2012); an exceptionally high rate of return.

According to the International Movement of People Affected by Vale, the company engages in 'strategic philanthropy' in order to 'please the public'. Examples include music festivals, and in Brazil a new lighting system for the famous statue of Christ in Rio de Janeiro. It spends around a billion dollars a year on 'corporate social responsibility activities'. However, its actions in relation to its business practices are more controversial. For example, its direct greenhouse gas emissions are calculated to have increased by 70 per cent from 2009 to 2010; and if its suppliers and consumers are included, many multiples of that (ibid.). The company, by itself, is thought consume 4 per cent of all the energy in Brazil. Furthermore, in 2010 there were eleven deaths of its workers on the job and:

> In Mozambique, for example, the Moatize mining mega project resulted in the removal of 760 of the 1,313 peasant farmer families registered for resettlement in a six month period between November 2009 and April 2010 to make way for the opening of coal mines. The company divided the families up between rural and semi-urban, using different criteria for resettlements. Families that were considered 'rural' were relocated 45 km from their community of origin and 75 km from the city of Tete. (ibid.: 6)

The Moatize coal project was awarded a lease, which can be renewed, for an area of 23,790 hectares for thirty-five years by the Mozambican government. The mine has an annual targeted output of between 8 and 10 million tonnes of metallurgical coal and 4 million tonnes of thermal coal (Campbell 2007), and this project will reportedly turn Mozambique into Africa's second-largest coal producer, behind only South Africa (Visentini 2010). It is estimated that by 2025 Tete Province in Mozambique could be producing a quarter of the world's coking coal (International Resource Journal n.d.).

Vale is conscious of its social licence to operate and 'in 2008, Vale requested SENAI to support the design of a training program to respond to the skilled-labour requirements for its carbon mine in the district of Moatize' (World Bank and IPEA 2011: 65). SENAI is a not-for-profit organization that trains skilled workers for industry.

According to the International Movement of People Affected by Vale (2012: 4), 'Vale conducts its activities through an integrated chain that links mines and steel factories to railway lines, railway lines to ports, and ports to maritime transport. Each stage of this process generates enormous social and environmental impacts, which need to be analysed in an integrated and coordinated way.' There is a cluster of twenty Brazilian companies working with Vale on the Moatize project, although the company also says that it has signed contracts with 439 companies that are registered in Mozambique (fin24 2012). There was also controversy over the use of Filipino and Brazilian workers on the project, who were reportedly paid more than locals, although the company says that 84 per cent of workers at the coal mine are from Mozambique (International Movement of People Affected by Vale 2012). The importation of foreign workers deepened the process of the translocalization of Tete.

In Cateme in 2012 residents rioted and blocked the transport of coal by Vale. They were protesting against the loss of their land in Moatize, their displacement to a village 45 kilometres away and lack of compensation and job opportunities. However, their displacement and grievances attracted very little international attention, with a local NGO having to pay to get some media coverage. Some have accused Vale of exercising undue influence on governments, and in 2007 BNDES changed its statutes to be able to give funding to the company's projects. According to the International Movement of People Affected by Vale (ibid.: 12), 'the dominance of a single economic agent – in this case, Vale – creates a kind of authoritarian paternalism, in which the company dictates the course of the local economy according to its own interests'. However, this fits with domestic Brazilian politics. Displacement by Brazilian TNCs is partly occluded by cooperative aspects of globalization, particularly aid.

Brazilian aid initiatives in Africa

There has been substantial continuity between Lula's administration and that of his successor, Dilma Rousseff, who visited Angola, Mozambique and South Africa during her first year in office. She stresses the importance of Brazil leaving 'a legacy to Africa' (World Bank and IPEA 2011). According to one report, nearly 60 per cent of Brazilian technical cooperation was directed to Africa in 2010, particularly in relation to tropical agriculture and medicine, energy, vocational training and social protection.

In recent years Brazil has become one of the world's largest aid donors (Economist 2010b). While official figures do not accurately or fully reflect the extent of aid (as it is not a member of the Organisation for Economic Co-operation and Development or its Development Assistance Committee, Brazil does not have a unified accounting system for resources allocated to foreign aid), it is estimated that Brazilian foreign aid increased threefold in 2006, from US$120 million to US$365 million. This figure increased further in 2007 to US$437 million (Ayllón Pino 2010), and in 2010, according to one estimate, Brazil's foreign aid commitments amounted to approximately US$1.2 billion (Economist 2010b). However, the precise figures are disputed. For example, in 2010 ABC (the Brazilian Cooperation Agency), which runs technical cooperation projects, had a budget of just US$30 million (ibid.), but it was estimated in one study that Brazilian institutions spent fifteen times more than ABC on technical assistance programmes. Humanitarian assistance was estimated to have increased twentyfold in just three years (ibid.), and while this growth is remarkable, only a proportion of this was directed to Africa.

According to White (2010: 228), 'certain programmes around conditional cash transfers, incentive-based education, commercial farming and renewable energy (to name a few) are now being actively exported to African countries in what Brazilians call a transfer of "social technology"'. As Brazil is not an OECD member, or a country that regularly engages with the OECD, details of cooperation initiatives are hard to locate, and ABC operates in an entirely responsive way, i.e. it only responds to requests for assistance from partner countries rather than seeking out projects to implement (Burges 2011). The fact that ABC is responsive rather than directive underlines the fact that there is no quid pro quo expected from Brazilian development assistance, although Burges (ibid.) does note that a 'higher level linkage' exists as aid is concentrated on Africa in order to build new, or revive old, relationships, particularly with Lusophone countries which potentially offer greater commercial or diplomatic advantages over the longer term. Brazilian aid to Africa is concentrated on the members of the Países Africanos de Língua Oficial Portuguesa – otherwise known as Palop, and made up of Mozambique, Angola, Cape Verde and São Tomé e Principe (Saravia 2012). Interestingly, trade with Lusophone African countries, outside of Angola, has been minimal to date (Seibert 2012).

Brazil cooperates with thirty-five countries in Africa. In fact, a recent OECD report lists Brazil as the number-one provider of SSC (Smith et al. 2010). 'In the Brazilian case we find an institutional structure that parallels those found in the North, but with a streamlined administrative approach operating free of OECD-DAC restraints. This has created a nimbleness that is allowing Brazil to pursue effective development cooperation programming in a manner that also supports the country's foreign policy agenda' (Burges 2011).

In Africa some of these projects include an experimental farm in Senegal, health system reform in Angola and a training programme for professionals in Mozambique. Another example of Brazilian cooperation listed by the OECD is the Brazilian-funded programme to support the cotton industry in Benin, Burkina Faso, Mali and Chad. This programme introduced Brazilian cotton plant strains to the four countries, with the aim of making cotton production more profitable. In Sotuba, Mali, where the new strains have been introduced, a 10 per cent increase in yields has been recorded (OECD 2011). In spite of Brazilian technological expertise in the area of cotton growing, the OECD report details how the programme places an emphasis on incorporation of local agricultural knowledge.

Brazil has also had similar programmes based on sharing of

expertise in Ghana, Kenya, Mozambique and Angola (International Policy Centre for Inclusive Growth 2009; UNDP 2008). These programmes involved Brazilian government officials with expertise in areas such as education, food security, juvenile justice and management visiting African countries and sharing their expertise through workshops and classes. The Brazilian Agricultural Research Corporation (EMBRAPA) has also been active in Africa through a variety of projects – for example, in Mali, where cotton yields at an experimental farm have increased dramatically (Economist 2010b).

The ABC is at the forefront of Brazil's foreign aid work. In Brazil, the term 'cooperation' is favoured over the term 'aid', as explained by head of the ABC Marco Farani: 'However, in Brazil, when we talk about aid, we are talking about cooperation: South–South Co-operation (SSC). This involves collaboration and knowledge-sharing through a horizontal structure, not the vertical structure that is at the core of developed countries' approaches and embodied in the terms "aid" and "assistance"' (Farani 2011).

However, as noted in the introduction, the discourse of 'South–South' cooperation serves to disguise continuing and deepening power inequality between partners. While relations between states may be characterized, in certain instances, by greater horizontality, this is not the case in relation to corporate investment and local populations.

The domestic politics of Brazil's Africa strategy

As noted earlier, the claim is sometimes made that Brazil has the second-highest number of Africans (people of African descent) in the world after Nigeria. Lula's foreign minister argued that 'with 76 million Afro-descendants ... [Brazil is] the second blackest nation in the world ... and [consequently] the government is committed to reflect this reality in its foreign politics' (quoted in Cicalo 2012: 12). The Brazilian foreign ministry, Itamaraty, now reserves 10 per cent of its job openings for 'black' applicants.

African cultural practices survived in Bahia (Brazil) and ancestral homes have been identified in Benin in West Africa, creating 'a remarkable cultural revival' (De Blij 2012: 318). The ancestors of most people of African descent were brought to Brazil as slaves, and around half of Brazil's population of 190 million people can trace African descent. While some claimed that the country was non-racial, unlike the United States, for example, this was never the case, even if there was less racism than elsewhere. According to Cicalo (2012: 1), 'Brazil today is increasingly spelling out its blackness ... at a historical moment when programs of "black" affirmative action and other differential policies in favour of Afro-descendants are taking off in Brazil, and also at a time when Brazil is expanding its geopolitical and economic interests in Africa, by and large under the sign of "South-South cooperation"'.

The idea that Brazil has a particular affinity with Africa has a long history. For example, it was a Brazilian sociologist, Gilberto Freyre, who developed the idea of Luso-tropicalism. This was the idea that the Portuguese were better and more humane colonizers in Africa and elsewhere than other powers because of their cultural and historical links, and affinity, with the continent. In relation to Brazil, Freyre wrote, 'Every Brazilian, even the light skinned fair haired one carries about him on his soul, when not on soul and body alike, the shadow or at least the birthmark of the aborigine or the negro, in our affections' (quoted in Louis Gates 2011: 43).[8] This imaginary prefigured ideas around hybridity and the imaginary of the 'Black Atlantic' developed by Gilroy (1993).

Brazil's 'blackness' provides a competitive advantage in Africa, as does the Portuguese language in 'Lusophone' parts of the continent. Good relations with Africa also serve to garner domestic political support among Brazil's 'black' population. President Lula argued that there was no way that Brazil could repay Africa its historical debt to it.

The rise of Brazil in Africa?

As democracy deepens its roots within the country, Brazil has attempted to link an increasingly activist stance in world affairs with political support at home for a more active partisan involvement in foreign policy. In this context, the government's fight against poverty and unequal income distribution at home and its assertive and activist foreign policy can be viewed as two sides of the same coin. (Soares de Lima and Hirst 2006: 21)

Soares and Hirst do not see any contradiction between Brazil's domestic and foreign policies. Brazil is one of the few countries in the world which has managed to reduce domestic income inequality in the context of neoliberal globalization and has also promoted a particular vision of cooperative globalization, bolstered by a rapidly expanding programme of aid or development cooperation. However, the expansion of its economy continues to be based substantially on the growth and geographic expansion of its transnational corporations.

There is a debate in the literature about whether or not such TNC-driven capital accumulation is inherently conflictive or not. However, it is clear in the Brazilian case that natural resource companies have been involved in displacement and inequality generation in 'host' countries in Africa. Their expansion can be seen to offer a partial 'spatial fix' to the conflict between labour and capital domestically in Brazil, despite the fact that rhetorically and discursively new aid initiatives and the discourse of 'blackness' facilitate their expansion. This is not to suggest that Brazilian foreign policy is conspiratorial or insincere, but rather that it is infused with multiple objectives, meanings and outcomes which vary by translocality.

Brazil's aid policies could be argued to serve underlying geo-strategic and economic objectives – as a veil for these. However, as Mann (1986) reminds us, social action results from 'polymorphous crystallisations' of varying motives and objectives and economic structures originate as ideas (Wendt 1999). The Brazilian state has arguably externalized elements of its domestic class compromise to Africa – promoting capital accumulation and redistribution. However, juridical independence in Africa and the differentiated geography of resources have given this a different context, as it is not necessarily associated with the rights of citizenship. Rather Brazilian investment has sometimes resulted in dispossession, at the same time as Brazilian-inspired social programmes are rolled out elsewhere.

Brazilian foreign policy is Janus faced, reflecting the contradictions described above. Under Lula, for example, his leftist special adviser on foreign affairs was designated to deal with 'ideological' issues such as relations with Venezuela, while the minister for foreign relations dealt with more 'technical issues', such as World

Trade Organization negotiations (Vigevani and Cepaluni 2009). This 'pragmatism' reflects a neostructuralist or dependency/neoliberal hybrid style of governance which is reflected in concrete outcomes in Africa, where Brazilian involvement arguably results in both poverty reduction and production through displacement by corporations, for example. The primary axis of engagement, however, appears to be around natural resource extraction and the extension of Brazil's own natural-resource-driven development, with all of the problems of sustainability associated with that.

As described above, Brazil is pursuing a multi-vector foreign policy in Africa, in common with the other BRICS powers. The country brings a number of advantages to its dealings with African states in terms of experience with poverty reduction, biofuel production and cultural links and affinities. However, it, and many of its companies, do not have the same power resources as China and its state-owned corporations. Consequently, Brazil is likely to remain a secondary power in Africa, except perhaps in 'Lusophone' countries, where its aid is being targeted and its companies have sometimes had 'first mover' advantages.

7 | CONCLUSION: GOVERNANCE AND THE EVOLUTION OF GLOBALIZATION IN AFRICA

The nature of globalization is rapidly evolving as the BRICS powers, in particular, assert their individual and collective power in world affairs. This is reflected both in international institutional fora, such as the G20, BRICS and IBSA, and in their bilateral relations with other states, as described in previous chapters. All of the BRICS states seek to consolidate a multipolar world order, as displacement of United States leadership in the near term is not possible given its military dominance, global reach, network of alliances and the weight of its economy (not adjusted for purchasing power parity). They all pursue a multi-vector foreign policy in Africa given their, to date, limited power resources, although the influence of China on the continent is now formidable. This influence derives from a number of sources, including 'polar power' in opposition to the United States, a shared history of exploitation by the Western powers and substantial economic and ideational resources around poverty reduction. Collectively, the BRICS powers largely agree on the outlines of what should constitute 'South Space', while their firms also compete economically. They also attempt to coordinate their positions in international fora, at least to some extent, to bolster their collective power.

The rise of the BRICS in Africa has resulted in a revision of the global governance template or matrix for the continent. Each of the BRICS powers in Africa is anxious to maintain open access for its investments and access to resources and markets, but they are less prescriptive and intrusive about the precise content of economic policy outside of these parameters, in contrast to the international financial institutions and previous approaches of Western donors. Furthermore, none of them seeks to apply political conditionality, with important implications for the nature of politics and development on the continent.

All of the BRICS, in contrast to Western powers, subscribe to a policy of non-interference in internal affairs, rhetorically, if not necessarily in practice. Brazil under President Lula had a declared policy of 'non-indifference' to human rights abuses, but in practice this did not amount to much, as the Brazilian government continued to develop and deepen ties with highly authoritarian regimes such as Zimbabwe. The downplaying of human rights and the primacy given to 'South–South' cooperation and solidarity reflects underlying strategic imperatives and also perhaps calculations about what the limits and potentialities of action are in a largely neoliberalized global political economy.

The BRICS powers can also provide material backing for their stance given their substantial foreign exchange reserves and deployment of innovative foreign policy instruments, as described in previous chapters. China has the largest foreign exchange reserves in the world at US$3.3 trillion (Bloomberg News 2012).

If (coercive) 'good governance' were the watchwords of the 1990s and 2000s, Western aid donors have now dramatically changed tack in an attempt to retain and build influence in Africa, with the British government now explicitly seeking to build its 'soft power' in aid relations, for example (United Kingdom Department for International Development 2011). The days of dictating to African governments are waning.

This dual reconfiguration of geo-governance – by the BRICS, and now by Western donors in response – opens up the prospect of greater autonomy for African states. However, it also carries the risk of strengthening extant authoritarian regimes. This concluding chapter assesses the prospects for governance in Africa in light of current trends, and explores whether or not the BRICS represent a coherent counter-pole to 'the West', which has dominated Africa's international relations for centuries.

Governance and the contradictions of South Space

The rise of the BRICS in Africa is a momentous event, even if it is replete with its own contradictions. For example, while 'horizontal' development cooperation is based on principles of greater equality, this may serve to occlude the continuing nature of unequal trade and investment with new 'partners'. Furthermore, the discourse of South–South globalization is one of rebalancing the global order and democratization, even as new institutions such as IBSA or BRICS, or relatedly the G20, inscribe new hierarchies.

'South Space' is a homogenized imaginary, whereas the reality is very different, characterized by huge power differentials and deeply uneven translocalization. Nonetheless, its discursive construction is now framing African development. It derives its power from growing material flows and its emotive and practical appeal to developing country state elites. It also derives it power from the political economy and failure of the previous development paradigm – World Bank/IMF structural adjustment.

Whereas 'structural adjustment' was enforced from the 'top down' by the World Bank and the International Monetary Fund, SSC is meant to be 'horizontal' in terms of power relations and consequently consensual, although relations of force, through structural power, or direct population displacement in the case of particular investments, still structure its actuality. The political economy of South Space is constructed through an emphasis on the rights of states. It eschews 'one size fits all' development models in favour of a gradualist and evolutionary approach to economic and political reform – 'crossing the river by feeling the stones', as the Chinese saying credited to Deng Xiaoping has it. Discursively in business and political fora, Africa is presented as a place of opportunity, although this disguises ongoing exploitation of people and (their) natural resources. Exploitation is the flip-side of opportunity, depending on where actors are positioned in global production networks and political structures.

The rise of the BRICS in Africa is also resulting in a reconfiguration of African states. 'The state' is not a thing, or a unified actor, but comprises sets of social relations infused with strategic calculus (Jessop 2008). The rise of the BRICS is resulting in a (dis)empowerment of African states, depending on and in relation to particular sets of actors. There are contradictions in this; even in relation to individual sets of actors. For example (some) African states are arguably being empowered through new sources of finance to resist World Bank/IMF diktats, even as they have had voting rights diluted in those institutions. African states are arguably being further empowered relative to their populations, even as their ecological space is being further colonized by (new) overseas-based actors.

Under the old Western-centred governance matrix African political elites were told/asked to liberalize both economically and politically. This generated a governance contradiction as incumbent governments were often reluctant to do the two together as 'shock therapy' was politically unpopular. This resulted in a mix of strategies whereby the extent to which structural adjustment policies were implemented was dependent on the power of the international financial institutions in particular countries versus popular accountability, and the opportunities economic reforms opened up for accumulation within the state apparatus (Gibbon 1996). The rise of the BRICS in Africa has resulted in a new dispensation whereby there is substantially less pressure for political liberalization, and relatedly economic liberalization, particularly in the context of relatively rapid economic growth, when tax revenues and public services are generally increasing.

African states vary in terms of 'extraversion portfolios', whereby they convert 'dependent relations with the external world into domestic resources and authority' (Peiffer and Englebert 2012: 355). What the rise of the BRICS partly does is to expand the portfolio of extraversion possibilities to enable regime maintenance. While the impacts of structural adjustment varied from case to case (and by releasing the foreign exchange constraint in post-conflict Uganda, for example, it sometimes resulted in substantial economic growth), in general the political economy formula of SAP approximated the one below.

Economic liberalization generates popular resistance (Gibbon et al. 1992); political liberalization creates an additional channel for this to be expressed, compromising regime maintenance. This resulted in a political structure characterized by sham or 'virtual' democracies, which often resisted (aspects of) imposed IMF reforms (Van de Walle 2001). The rise of the BRICS has resulted in a different formula, which can be concisely expressed as:

Revived economic growth and tax revenues + aid + 'no questions asked' = (in general) regime maintenance.

While the average number of years in power for African leaders has been falling since the 1960s (Theron 2011), they still tend to spend longer in power than counterparts in other world regions, and it will be interesting to see how the rise of the BRICS on the continent affects this trend.

The fundamental extraversion of African economies and politics remains unchanged as the continent remains primarily a recipient of limited and natural-resource-concentrated foreign direct investment, an aid recipient and an exporter of primary commodities. The nature of this extraversion has changed as the current 'commodity super-cycle' has revived economic growth and resource scarcity has made Africa a geopolitico-economic 'battleground' for the Great Powers. Also, African state actors have substantial agency in these processes in the choice of partners, as the previous chapters demonstrated. This has implications for the reconfiguring nature of power in the international political economy.

'Soft power' and 'hard power' are two-way streets. While stronger powers may have greater leverage in target countries, they are also influenced by their foreign entanglements and new reverse depend-encies and cultural and other flows are created. As energy becomes more scarce, energy-rich countries have greater influence in world affairs in particular. These processes could be read as a deepening of the process of globalization, which it is. But it plays out very unevenly and is perhaps better captured as a process of translocalization char-acterized by selective linkages and differentiation, described earlier. This deepening translocalization between the BRICS and other powers and Africa is paralleled by a process of trans*national*ization, whereby ideas and policy programmes designed in Washington by the World Bank and the IMF become less influential, and binational ideational flows from the BRICS and elsewhere become more important.

More fundamentally, the rise of the BRICS in Africa, and China in particular, is undermining the very notion of 'the West'. Some have argued that the West is defined by adherence to the wishes of the United States government. The devastation wrought by the Second World War in Europe and the US role in underwriting the peace economically, politically and militarily gave it a unique power on that continent. Even with increasing European integration the USA was able to dominate individual countries. However, 'the West' is partly defined by its other. The rise of China in Africa is undermining the idea of the West as 1) 'all powerful', 2) beneficent and charitable and 3) the source and site of knowledge production. This, combined with the GFC, is resulting in a 'Southization' of the global North, as a number of countries in Europe suffer under IMF/EU-imposed/ designed austerity programmes (Lewis 2011b; see also Comaroff and Comaroff 2012).

The failure of the neoliberal model and the economic success of developmental states in Asia and also in Brazil has resulted in a stalling of neoliberalization in Africa, although the fundamentals of free trade and international capital mobility are constitutional-ized through the World Trade Organization in particular (Gill 2008). Transnational capital, irrespective of its national origin, also seeks out favourable geographical locales for its expanded reproduction, with more 'open' policy regimes often as an implicit conditionality of capitalization.

While each of the BRICS powers is partially driven by economic motives for expansion into Africa, their governments are also driven by domestic political concerns, particularly regime maintenance, and relatedly power and international respect enhancement. The political regime in each of the different powers is different, ranging from social democratic (Brazil) to 'market Stalinism' (China) (Henderson 1993), but some of the impetus remains the same along this dimension. Each of the BRICS powers is also anxious to bolster its international sovereignty and foreign alliances also serve this goal, through support in the United Nations General Assembly, for example.

Various opinion polls and studies show that, in general, African populations tend to have more favourable views of Chinese invest-ment than not, sometimes of the order of two to one (Moyo 2012). However, this may change as its volume increases. The contributions in Fraser and Larmer (2010) explore the tension between copper as a 'national resource' and an 'international commodity' in Zambia. Ownership and the distribution of costs and benefits which arise from its extraction have generated social and political tensions, including, at times, riots and kidnappings. However, Zambia may be somewhat exceptional in the sense that there are strong memories of (relative) prosperity and 'expectations of modernity' (Ferguson 1999) associated with copper extraction from the 1960s. While the withdrawal of food subsidies, and increases in fuel costs under the auspices of World Bank/IMF structural adjustment programmes (Walton and Seddon 1994), often generated instability in Africa, the deepening process of translocalization may mean that some conflict, such as the riots in Mozambique described earlier, is more localized. However, the global commodity super-cycle, substantially driven by the BRICS, has pushed food prices dramatically higher, which also resulted in riots across Africa and in Mozambique in particular in 2010 (Economist 2010c). Also, the largely extractive nature of the BRICS' engagements with Africa is likely to generate further tensions, even if relatively high rates of economic growth and transnational elite pacting have largely repressed these for the moment.

As has been described in the book, the different BRICS powers have different interests and strategies in Africa. The two BRICS powers that exert the strongest governance influence on the continent at the moment are China and South Africa – globally the strongest and weakest members of the group. This relates to both levels of investment and also the fact that South African interests are increasingly aligned with those of China. South Africa's gregional power configuration means that it also serves as a transmission belt for global forces to the rest of the continent. It is probably not accurate to refer to geo-governance at national levels by the other members of the group, although their companies and conglomerates may exercise substantial control at local level, as described in the book. However, collectively the BRICS policy of 'non-interference' facilitates power projection and influence in investment and trade in particular.

Local-level dispossession associated with investment from the different BRICS powers and their other more poverty-reducing initiatives mean they can be characterized as globalizing (under)developmental states or simply capitalist states, despite their different political economies and complexions. The long-term impacts of the rise of the BRICS in Africa is uncertain as revived economic growth holds out the potential for the reinscription of the dialectics of capitalist development, as stronger working and middle classes may have more power to hold domestic states to account. However, the 'liberal' neo-Westphalian bargain between the BRICS powers and incumbent

African political classes would suggest that the power of incumbent elites is being strengthened. From 2008 to mid-2012, ten of the thirteen leaders of countries who died in office were in Africa (Alexander 2012). Many African leaders have been in power for decades – for example, President Obiang in Equatorial Guinea, who came to power in 1979, or Robert Mugabe in Zimbabwe, who came to power in 1980. Thus, the broad structure of African political economy – economic extraversion coupled with often authoritarian governance – is likely to remain largely intact in the medium term at least. However, in contrast to the recent past this configuration is now compatible with economic growth, driven largely by higher global commodity prices. The eleven largest African countries have a collective economy equivalent in size to that of India or Russia (O'Neill 2011).

In terms of global geopolitics, some have questioned whether the BRICS will continue to grow in influence (Sharma 2012). Sharma notes that Brazil and Russia's economic growth halved, approximately, from 2008, and India's fell by a third. However, these growth performances still put them ahead of many countries in the developed world which often suffered severe economic contractions. Also in terms of economic weight, China's economy was still only one third the size of that of the USA at the end of 2010, when not adjusted for purchasing power parity (O'Neill 2011). However, current structural dynamics point to the continued growth and growing geopolitical importance of the BRICS. First, global natural resource scarcity would appear likely to intensify, benefiting countries such as Russia, which is the world's largest energy exporter, Brazil and South Africa.[1] Furthermore, both China and India maintained rapid, if reduced, economic growth during the global financial crisis, based on the diversification and deepening of their economies. Moreover, the Triffin dilemma, whereby the issuer of the global reserve currency, which is still the USA, has to run trade deficits in order to finance demand for its currency, still operates. While the USA is keen to retain this role, given the higher living standards it entails by simply being able to print money to import goods from overseas (Cohen 2000), it does create economic imbalances and demand which favour the continued growth of China in particular, barring another major global financial crisis.

Geo-governance, or power projection across political borders, is not just a phenomenon occurring in Africa. Africa's relative marginality in previous decades, plus its natural resources, made it an obvious target of Chinese and other BRICS power interest. However, China's influence, in particular, is now extending worldwide, with plans to build a Chinese wholesale hub in Ireland to serve the European market, for example. Comaroff and Comaroff (2012) describe the ways in which they think that 'Euro-America' may be evolving towards Africa. The rapidly growing influence of the BRICS powers, and China in particular, in Africa may portend the future for other world regions.

NOTES

1 Introduction

1 At PPP. It is classed as an upper-middle-income (developing) country by the World Bank for lending purposes, however.

2 This included, perhaps on the theory that 'my enemy's enemy is my friend', UNITA in Angola.

3 In 2011 Chinese companies began building a surveillance facility for the Zimbabwean government which would reportedly monitor internet traffic and opposition leaders' phone calls.

4 Although there is also a history of inspiration and interaction between the diaspora in the United States and Africa, as expressed through rap music, for example (Osumare 2012).

2 China

1 This chapter draws on 'Globalisation and the Rise of the State? Chinese Geogovernance in Zambia', *New Political Economy*, 17(2), 2012: 209–30, www.tandfonline.com

2 Consequently the term geo-governance is preferred to imperialism.

3 Governance is always geographical but for the purposes of this chapter it becomes geo-governance when it transcends the national scale. We are grateful to James Sidaway for encouraging us to develop this point.

4 We are grateful to Patricia Ehrkamp for this point.

5 It does, however, insist that it will have diplomatic relations only with countries which do not recognize the Republic of China (Taiwan).

6 For a fuller history of TAZARA, see Monson (2009).

7 The governments of Tanzania and Zambia are currently in discussions about privatizing TAZARA, given dramatic reductions in freight on the line.

8 Interview with manager, 8 August 2009.

9 Of course, the Chinese also continue to build roads in Zambia.

10 Interview, 8 August 2009.

11 P. Honohan, personal communication, 25 August 2009.

12 Interview, S. Mulonda and N. Muyambango, 5 August 2009.

13 Field notes, August 2009.

14 P. Honohan, personal communication, 2009.

15 Interview, B. Ngula, board trustee, Zambia Congress of Trade Unions, 5 August 2009.

16 Interview, C. Sifafula, 5 August 2009.

17 Confidential interview at copper smelter, August 2009; Taylor (2006).

18 The Japanese government is continuing to support the development of a Lusaka South MFEZ (see JICA 2007).

19 Interview with R. Banda, 5 August 2009.

20 Interview, Collins, 2009.

21 Interview, S. Mulonda and N. Muyambango, 2009.

22 Ibid. However, he saw the overall impacts of Chinese investment as positive and said that, particularly by promoting competition in the construction sector, it was a 'wake-up call for Zambian companies'.

23 Interview, P. Kalasa and M. Amukusana, 10 August 2009.

24 This is a unit of CNMC.

25 Interview, Ngula, 2009.

26 Ibid.

27 Confidential interview, August 2009.

28 Interview, 14 August 2009.

29 We are grateful to Paul Walsh for this point.

30 Interview at Sino-Zambian Friendship Hospital, 10 August 2009.

31 Interview with chief medical officer, Sino-Zambian Friendship Hospital, 10 August 2009.

32 Sata had threatened to recognize Taiwan over Beijing if he was elected, leading the Chinese ambassador to state that if he was elected diplomatic and economic relations would be severed. Since then Sata has toned down his previous inflammatory rhetoric and argued that large-scale Chinese investment which created jobs was welcome in Zambia.

33 Poster of the Anhui Foreign Economic Construction Group (AFECG), Ndola, 11 August 2009.

34 Interview, S. Mulonda and N. Muyambango, 2009.

35 Interview, 11 August 2009.

36 Interview, 15 August 2009.

37 Interview, 11 August 2009.

38 Interview, 10 August 2009.

39 Interview, 8 August 2009.

40 Interview, S. Mulonda and N. Muyambango, 2009.

41 Interview with International Labour Organization official, 13 August 2009.

42 Interview, 12 August 2009.

43 Confidential interview, Lusaka, August 2009.

44 Confidential interview, August 2009.

45 According to the new Zambian minister of finance, 'China's economy is vital not only to Zambia and Africa but the whole globe as well. We value this cooperation because you have come to our aid in our time of need such as the construction of the TAZARA. This is among the many achievements we have recorded as a country through this strengthened friendship' (Chikwanda, quoted in Namusa 2012).

3 South Africa

1 This chapter draws on 'Another BRIC in the wall? South Africa's developmental impact and contradictory rise in Africa and beyond', *European Journal of Development Research*, 24(2), 2012, pp. 223–41.

2 There has also been a scandal recently about the amount of public money used to refurbish President Zuma's residence in his home region. The upgrade cost the equivalent of almost twenty million pounds sterling.

3 This is a subsidiary of Associated British Foods.

4 IMF 2009, reported in Scott, personal communication, October 2012.

5 Interview with employee, Chambishi Special Economic Zone, Zambia, August 2009.

6 Interview, Durban, South Africa, July 2010.

4 India

1 This chapter draws on my chapter in Tony Allan et al. (eds), *The Handbook of Water and Land Grabs in Africa*, Routledge, London and New York, 2012.

2 Climate change could also result in other countries seeking to purchase land in India. For example, as his country is inundated by rising sea water, the president of the Maldives is looking to purchase land for the population of that country in either India or Sri Lanka (Zoomers 2011).

5 Russia

1 This was continued during the 'interregnum' of Medvedev's premiership from 2008 to 2012, when Putin remained the power behind the throne.

2 Although in the context of the eurozone crisis he was subsequently supplanted by Angela Merkel, the German Chancellor.

3 At that time the US Secretary of State, Condoleezza Rice, reportedly said that US policy would be to 'punish France, ignore Germany and forgive Russia' (BBC 2005). Russia's large strategic nuclear arsenal made it too important for a realist like Rice to antagonize (Heilbrunn 2012).

4 Although others question whether he was awarded this degree, and there have also been allegations of plagiarism.

5 In the case of Somalia, it switched sides between the superpowers in order to try to leverage benefits and bolster the regime's survival. The withdrawal of American military support with the end of the Cold War was one of the reasons the state collapsed in 1991.

6 Although, more recently Russian economic power has revived.

7 Others also note that the operational efficiency of Russian mining is low. 'Out of the 14 major minerals, only gas, uranium and diamond reserves are exploited at a level of over 50%' (Vassiliev 2011).

8 Rumours circulate as to Vladimir Putin's net worth. His associates have certainly grown wealthy under his rule (Kramer and Herszenhorn 2012). According to a recent survey the Russian population regard President Putin's government as halfway between a democracy and a dictatorship (Rose 2012).

9 BRICS cooperation includes military affairs, as India recently leased a nuclear submarine from Russia, although China has recently reduced Russian arms imports in order to develop its own capabilities.

6 Brazil

1 In particular, primary products for the first time now account for a greater share of Brazil's exports than manufactured goods (beyondbrics 2010). This has been largely driven by trade with China, which exerts demand for raw materials and deindustrializing pressures on Brazilian manufacturers.

2 Although interestingly South Africa has recently dramatically increased duties on Brazilian chicken exports, claiming that they were being dumped in that country. This case is now being tried before the WTO. The South African government is obviously not as wary of alienating Brazil as it is of alienating China, given its far greater economic importance for the country.

3 By some estimates Petrobras is the fourth-largest publicly traded energy company in the world, although the Brazilian government still owns the majority stake. It had the world's largest share offering ever, of US$67 billion, in September 2010 (O'Neill 2011).

4 In parts of Africa, Brazilian evangelical churches are also growing strongly. In South Africa alone there are over three hundred temples of the Igreja Universal do Reino de Deus (Visentini 2010). The World Mission of the Batiste Congregation is active in fifteen African countries.

5 Although it should be noted that Lula allowed Petrobras to play economic 'hardball' with Bolivia, which in the end meant that the only substantial gain to Bolivia was that Brazil paid a small premium on the gas (Burges 2009).

6 The MDGs measure progress relative to the situation in 1990.

7 The regionality index is the percentage of host countries in a world

region in which a Brazilian company is located as a percentage of all of the countries in which it has operations, times one hundred.

8 While Freyre was very influential and his work contributed to the making of a distinctively less racial Brazilian identity, the idea of Luso-tropicalism served to cover up heinous Portuguese colonial policies in Africa, such as forcing women to pick a certain amount of cotton by leaving their babies in boxes out in the sun in what is now Mozambique (Hanlon 1996).

7 Conclusion

1 Although some projections suggest that the USA will become energy independent by mid-century as a result of oil extraction from shale fields. Futhermore, 'urban mining', where metal is retrieved and recycled from existing products, may reduce metals demand in the future.

BIBLIOGRAPHY

Adebajo, A. (2008) 'Hegemony on a shoestring: Nigeria's post-Cold War foreign policy', in A. Adebajo and A. Mustapha (eds), *Gulliver's Troubles: Nigeria's Foreign Policy after the Cold War*, Scottsville: University of KwaZulu-Natal Press, pp. 1–37.

— (2010) *The Curse of Berlin: Africa after the Cold War*, New York: Columbia University Press.

Adebajo, A., A. Adedeji and C. Landsberg (2007) 'Introduction', in A. Adebajo, A. Adedeji and C. Landsberg (eds), *South Africa in Africa: The Post-Apartheid Era*, Durban: University of KwaZulu-Natal Press, pp. 17–39.

AFECG (Anhui Foreign Economic Construction Group) (2010) www.afecc.com/en/about.asp?second_id=11006, accessed 17 May 2009.

Africa Europe Faith and Justice Network (2010) 'Arms exports and transfers: Europe to Africa, by country', www.aefjn.org/tl_files/aefjn-files/arms/arms_material%20eng/1101AEFJN ReportArmsAfrica_Africa_eng.pdf.

Africa Report (2011) *Top 500 Companies in Africa*, www.africareport.com.

Africa–South America Cooperation Forum (2006) 'Partnership in energy under the ASA Cooperation Framework', www.african-union.org.

African Development Bank (2011) 'Russia's economic engagement with Africa', *African Economic Brief*, 2.

Alden, C. (2005) 'Leveraging the dragon: toward "An Africa that can say no"', *YaleGlobal Online Magazine*, yaleglobal.yale.edu/content/leveraging-dragon-toward-africa-can-say-no, accessed 12 September 2009.

— (2009) 'Emerging powers and Africa: a comparison of modes of engagement by China, India and Brazil', *Global Review*, pp. 62–74.

Alden, C. and G. Le Pere (2009) 'South Africa in Africa: bound to lead?', *Politikon*, 36(1): 145–69.

Alexander, R. (2012) 'Why do so many African leaders die in office?', *BBC New Magazine*, www.bbc.co.uk/news/magazine-19356410.

Alinyeju, O. (2012) 'Enter the tiger', *African Business*, 391: 70–1.

Allan, J. A. (1998) 'Virtual water: a strategic resource global solution to regional deficits', *Ground Water*, 36(4): 545–6.

Amazon Watch, International Rivers (2012) 'Brazilian mining giant Vale voted worst corporation in the world', www.internationalrivers.org/resources/brazilian-mining-giant-vale-voted-worst-corporation-in-the-world-3690.

Andreasson, S. (2010) *Africa's Development Impasse: Rethinking the Political Economy of Transformation*, London: Zed Books.

Angola Press (2012) 'President congratulates Portuguese, Russian counterparts', www.portalangop.co.ao/motix/en_us/noticias/politica/2012/5/24/President-congratulates-Portuguese-Russian-counterparts,5bc72ac4-0305-4f08-84cf-1ce608170c18.html.

Appadurai, A. (1995) 'The production of locality', in R. Fardon (ed.), *Counterworks: Managing the diversity of knowledge*, New York: Routledge, pp. 204–25.

— (1996) *Modernity at Large: Cultural dimensions of globalisation*, Minneapolis and London: University of Minnesota Press.

Armijo, L. E. (2007) 'The BRICS countries (Brazil, Russia, India, and China) as analytical category: mirage or insight?', *Asian Perspective*, 31(4): 7–42.

Arnold, G. (2009) *The New Scramble for Africa*, London: North South Books.

Arrighi, G. (2007) *Adam Smith in Beijing: Lineages of the Twenty First Century*, New York and London: Verso.

AsiaPulse News (2008) 'India seeks African diamonds: Ramesh to visit Angola, Namibia', *AsiaPulse News*, 24 March.

Ayllón Pino, B. (2010) 'Brazilian cooperation: a model under construction for an emerging power (ARI)', www.realinstitutoelcano.org/wps/portal/rielcano_eng/Content? WCM_GLOBAL_CONTEXT=/elcano/elcano_in/zonas_in/cooperation+developpment/ari143-2010, accessed 10 July 2012.

Badrinath, R. (2011) 'Karuturi to outsource Ethiopian land to Indian farmers', *Business Standard*, www.business-standard.com, 12 October.

Bair, J. and M. Werner (2011) 'The place of disarticulation: global commodity production in La Laguna, Mexico', *Environment and Planning A*, 43: 998–1015.

Barber, J. P. (2004) *Mandela's World: The International Dimension of South Africa's Political Revolution 1990–99*, Oxford/Cape Town/Athens: James Currey/David Philip/Ohio University Press.

Barbosa, A. D., T. Narciso and M. Biancalana (2009) 'Brazil in Africa: another emerging power in the continent?', *Politikon*, 36(1): 59–86.

Bariyo, N. and D. Maylie (2011) 'Zambia lifts ban on copper exports', *Wall Street Journal*, online.wsj.com/article/SB100014240529702034768045766 14214163979424.html.

Barka, B. and K. Mlambo (2011) 'India's economic engagement with Africa', *Africa Economic Brief*, 2(6): African Development Bank.

Barma, N., G. Chiozza, E. Ratner and S. Weber (2007) 'A world without the West? Empirical patterns and theoretical implications', *Chinese Journal of International Politics*, 2(4): 525–44.

Barnard, R. and G. Farred (2004) *After the Thrill is Gone: A Decade of Post-apartheid South Africa*, Durham, NC: Duke University Press.

Basu, K., S. De, R. Ghosh and Shweta (2011) *The Evolving Dynamics of Global Economic Power in the Post-Crisis World: Revelations from a New Index of Government Economic Power*, www.kaushikbasu.org/Index%20of%20Government%20Economic%20Power.pdf.

Basu, P. (2007) 'Political economy of land grab', *Economic and Political Weekly*, pp. 1281–7.

Baumgart, W. (1987) 'German imperialism in historical perspective', in A. J. Knoll and Lewis H. Gann (eds), *Germans in the Tropics: Essays in German Colonial History*, Westport, CT: Greenwood Press.

BBC (2005) 'Can Rice's trip heal rift with Europe', news.bbc.co.uk/2/hi/americas/4231895.stm.

— (2009a) 'Azprom seals $2.5bn Nigeria deal', news.bbc.co.uk/2/hi/business/8118721.stm.

— (2009b) 'Medvedev seeks closer African links', news.bbc.co.uk/2/hi/8113385.stm.

Beck, U. (1992) *Risk Society: Towards a New Modernity*, London and Newbury Park, CA: Sage.

Beijing Review (2009) 'Luo Guan and the prevention of graft', *Beijing Review*, 52.

Bello, W. (2009) *The Food Wars*, London: Verso.

Bessis, S. (2003) *Western Supremacy: Triumph of an Idea?*, London: Zed Books.

beyondbrics (2010) 'Chart of the week: Brazil's shifting export structure', *Financial Times*, November, blogs. ft.com.

Bilal, S. and F. Rampa (2011) 'Emerging economies in Africa and the development effectiveness debate', *Discussion Chapter 107*, Maastricht: ECDPM.

Billington, J. H. (2004) *Russia: In Search of Itself*, Baltimore, MD: Johns Hopkins University Press.

Blair, T. (2008) 'Faith and globalisation', Lecture, tonyblairoffice. org/2008/04/speech-on-faith-globalisation.html.

Bloomberg News (2012) 'China's slowing revenue gains seen limiting spending', www.bloomberg.com/news/2012-10-28/china-s-slowing-revenue-gains-seen-limiting-spending.html.

BNDES (2012) 'BNDES and Bradesco sign a contract to finance exports to Africa and Latin America', www.bndes.gov.br/SiteBNDES/bndes/bndes_en/Institucional/Press/Destaques_Primeira_Pagina/20120528_bradesco.html.

Boamah, P. B. (2011) 'Competition between biofuel and food? Evidence from a jatropha biodiesel project in Northern Ghana', in P. Matondi, K. Havenevik and A. Beyene (eds), *Biofuels, Land Grabbing and Food Security in Africa*, London: Zed Books, pp. 159–75.

Bond, P. (2004) *Talk Left, Walk Right: South Africa's Frustrated Global Reforms*, Durban: University of KwaZulu-Natal Press.

— (2006a) 'Zimbabwe, South Africa and the IMF', in *South African Yearbook of International Affairs 2005/2006*, Johannesburg: South African Institute of International Affairs.

— (2006b) *Looting Africa: The Economics of Exploitation*, Scottsville/London: University of KwaZulu-Natal Press/Zed Books.

Bond, P. and Zapiro (2006) *Talk Left, Walk Right: South Africa's Frustrated Global Reforms*, Scottsville: University of KwaZulu-Natal Press.

Bonilla, L. (2012) 'Brazil in major Africa investment and technology transfer plan', *Africa Review*, www.africareview.com/Business---Finance/Brazil-pledges-major-Africa-investment-drive/-/979184/1399404/-/13900u9/-/index.html.

Borras, S. and J. Franco (n.d.) 'From threat to opportunity? Problems with the idea of a "Code of Conduct" for land-grabbing', *Yale Human Rights and Development Law Journal*, 13: 507–23.

Bosshard, P. (2008) 'Zambia: from the World Bank to China and back', www.internationalrivers.org.

Bouzarovksi, S. and M. Bassin (2011) 'Energy and identity: imagining Russia as a hydrocarbon superpower', *Annals of the Association of American Geographers*, 101(4): 783–94.

Bowles, P. (2002) 'Regionalism and development after (?) financial crises', in S. Breslin, C. Hughes, N. Phillips and B. Rosamond (eds), *New Regionalisms in the Global Political Economy*, London: Routledge.

Brautigam, D. (2009) *Dragon's Gift: The Real Story of China in Africa*, Oxford: Oxford University Press.

Brautigam, D., T. Farole and T. Xiaoyang (2010) 'China's investment in

African special economic zones: prospects, challenges, and opportunities', Washington, DC, World Bank, vle.worldbank.org/bnpp/en/publications/trade/china-s-investment-african-special-economic-zones-prospects-challenges-and-opport.

Breslin, S. (2007) *China and the Global Political Economy*, New York: Palgrave Macmillan.

BRICS (2012) *The BRICS Report*, New Dehli: Oxford University Press.

Broadman, H. G. and G. Isik (2007) *Africa's Silk Road: China and India's New Economic Frontier*, Washington, DC: World Bank.

Brooks, A. (2010) 'Spinning and weaving discontent: labour relations and the production of meaning at Zambia–China Mulungushi Textiles', *Journal of Southern African Studies*, 36(1): 113–32.

Bukkvoll, T. (2003) 'Putin's strategic partnership with the West: the domestic politics of Russian foreign policy', *Comparative Strategy*, 22(3): 223–42.

Burawoy, M. (2000) *Global Ethnography: Forces, Connections, and Imaginations in a Postmodern World*, Berkeley: University of California Press.

Burges, S. W. (2007) 'Building a Global Southern Coalition: the competing approaches of Brazil's Lula and Venezuela's Chavez', *Third World Quarterly*, 28(7): 1343–58.

— (2008) 'Consensual hegemony: theorizing Brazilian foreign policy after the Cold War', *International Relations*, 22(1): 65–84.

— (2009) *Brazilian Foreign Policy after the Cold War*, Gainesville: University Press of Florida.

— (2011) 'Brazilian international development cooperation: budgets, procedures and issues with engage-ment', *Global Studies Review*, www.globality-gmu.net/archives/2726/print/.

Büscher, B. (2012) 'Spaces of investment and dispossession: notes on recent dynamics in the Southern African political economy of energy', Paper presented at the III Conferência do IESE.

Business News Americas (2008) 'Lula launches new production develop-ment policy – Brazil', *Business News Americas*, www.bnamericas.com.

Campbell, C. (2003) *Letting Them Die: Why HIV/AIDS Intervention Pro-grammes Fail*, Oxford: International African Institute.

Campbell, K. (2007) 'Brazil has "political, moral and historical obligation" to Africa – Brazilian president', *Mining Weekly*, www.miningweekly.com/article/brazil-has-political-moral-and-historical-obligation-to-africa-brazilian-president-2007-10-26.

— (2011) 'Vale aiming to invest $2 bn in Africa in the coming year', www.miningweekly.com/article/brazilian-group-reveals-2012-investment-plans-for-africa-2011-12-09.

Captain, Y. (2010) 'Brazil's Africa policy under Lula', *Global South*, 4(1): 183–98.

Carmody, P. (2007) *Neoliberalism, Civil Society and Security in Africa*, Basingstoke and New York: Palgrave Macmillan.

— (2010) *Globalisation in Africa: Re-colonization or renaissance*, Boulder, CO: Lynne Rienner.

— (2011a) *The New Scramble for Africa*, Cambridge: Polity.

— (2011b) 'India and the "Asian Drivers" in Africa', in E. Mawdsley and G. McCann (eds), *India in Africa: Changing geographies of power*, Cape Town: Pambazuka Press.

— (2011c) 'The scramble for timber and

biofuels in Africa', *Whitehead Journal of Diplomacy and International Relations*, XII(1): 125–36.

Carmody, P. and G. Hampwaye (2010) 'Inclusive or exclusive globalisation? Asian investment and Zambia's economy', *Africa Today*, 56(3): 84–102.

Carmody, P. and F. Owusu (2007) 'Competing hegemons? Chinese vs. American geoeconomic strategies in Africa', *Political Geography*, 26(5): 504–24.

Carmody, P. and I. Taylor (2010) 'Flexigemony and force in China's resource diplomacy in Africa', *Geopolitics*, 20(15): 1–20.

Cason, J. W. and T. J. Power (2009) 'Presidentialization, pluralization, and the rollback of Itamaraty: explaining change in Brazilian foreign policy making in the Cardoso–Lula era', *International Political Science Review*, 30(2): 117–40.

Centre for Chinese Studies (2007) 'Outcomes of the South Africa–China Bi-National Commission', *China Monitor*, 23, www.ccs.org.za/?p=1410.

Chahoud, T. (2008) 'Financing for development series: Southern non-DAC actors in development cooperation', in *DIE Briefing*, ch. 13.

Chaturvedi, S., T. Fues et al. (2012) *Development Cooperation and Emerging Powers: New partners or old patterns?*, London: Zed Books.

Chellah, G. (2010) 'Miners will have last laught over Rupiah – Sata', *The Post*.

Cheru, F. and M. Calais (2010) 'Countering new imperialisms: what role for the New Partnership for Africa's Development?', in F. Cheru and C. Obi (eds), *The Rise of China and India in Africa*, London and Uppsala: Zed Books and Nordiska Afrikainstitutet, pp. 221–42.

Cheru, F. and C. Obi (eds) (2010) *The Rise of China and India in Africa*, London and Uppsala: Zed Books and the Nordiska Afrikainstitutet.

Chestnut, S. and A. I. Johnston (2009) 'Is China rising?', in E. Paus, J. W. Western and P. B. Prime (eds), *Global Giants: Is China Changing the Rules of the Game?*, New York: Palgrave Macmillan, pp. 237–60.

Chossudovsky, M. (2002) *War and Globalisation: The Truth Behind 9/11*, Oakland, CA: Global Outlook Publishers.

Cicalo, A. (2012) 'Brazil and its African mirror: discussing "black" approximations in the South Atlantic', Working Paper no. 24, desiguALdades.net, Research Network on Interdependent Inequalities in Latin America.

Clark, D. (2012) *Africa's Future: Darkness to Destiny: How the Past is Shaping Africa's Economic Evolution*, London: Profile Books.

Clark, J. (2002) 'Museveni's adventure in the Congo war: Uganda's Vietnam', in J. Clark (ed.), *The African Stakes in the Congo War*, Basingstoke and New York: Palgrave Macmillan, pp. 145–68.

CNBC (2012) 'China overtakes Japan in Fortune Global 500 companies for first time', www.cnbc.com/id/48128996/China_Overtakes_Japan_in_Fortune_Global_500_Companies_for_First_Time.

Cohen, A. (2009) 'Russia's new scramble for Africa', *Wall Street Journal*, online.wsj.com/article/SB124639219666775441.html.

Cohen, B. (2000) *The Geography of Money*, Ithaca, NY: Cornell University Press.

Coker, C. (1985) *Nato, the Warsaw Pact and Africa*, London: Macmillan.

Collier, P. (2010) *The Plundered Planet: How to Reconcile Prosperity and Nature*, London: Allen Lane.

Comaroff, J. and J. Comaroff (2012) *Theory from the South: Or, How Euro-*

America is Evolving towards Africa, Boulder, CO: Paradigm.

Copson, R. (2007) *The United States in Africa: Bush Policy and Beyond*, London and Cape Town: Zed Books and David Phillips.

Cornelissen, S. (2009) 'Awkward embraces: emerging and established powers and the shifting fortunes of Africa's international relations in the twenty-first century', *Politikon*, 36(1): 5–26.

Cornelissen, S., F. Cheru and T. M. Shaw (2011) 'Introduction: Africa and international relations in the 21st century', in S. Cornelissen, F. Cheru and T. M. Shaw, *Africa and International Relations in the 21st Century*, Basingstoke and New York: Palgrave Macmillan, pp. 1–20.

Crush, J., B. Dodson, J. Gay, T. Green and C. Leduka (2010) 'Migration, remittances and "development" in Lesotho', Southern African Migration Programme working chapter, idasa.wordpress.com/2010/07/14/migration-remittances-and-development-in-lesotho-migration-policy-chapter-52/.

Daily Mail (2011) 'Brazil to build nuclear submarines which will dramatically alter balance of power in South America', *Daily Mail*, www.dailymail.co.uk/news/article-2015731/Brazil-build-nuclear-submarines-dramatically-alter-balance-power-South-America.html.

Damina Advisors (2012) 'Africa "week ahead"', 8–15 May, danquahinstitute.org/docs/Damina%20Newsletter%208%20-%2015%20May.pdf.

Daniel, J. (2006) 'South Africa in Africa: trends and forecasts in a changing African political economy', in G. Gunnarsen, P. MacManus, M. Nielson and H. E. Stolten (eds), *At the End of the Rainbow? Social identity and*
welfare state in the new South Africa, Copenhagen: South Africa Contact.

Daniel, J. and N. Bhengu (2009) 'South Africa in Africa: still a formidable player', in R. Southhall and H. Melber (eds), *A New Scramble for Africa? Imperialism, Investment and Development*, Durban: University of KwaZula-Natal Press, pp. 139–64.

Daniel, J., V. Naidoo and S. Naidu (2003) 'The South Africans have arrived: post-apartheid corporate expansion into Africa', in J. Daniel, A. Habib and R. Southall (eds), *State of the Nation: South Africa 2003–2004*, Cape Town: HSRC Press.

Darbouche, H. (2007) 'Russian–Algerian cooperation and the "gas OPEC": what's in the pipeline?', Centre for European Policy Studies.

Davies, M. (n.d.) 'Brazil as a newcomer in Africa'.

— (2008) 'Special economic zones: China's developmental model comes to Africa', in R. I. Rotberg (ed.), *China into Africa: Trade, aid and influence*, Cambridge, MA, and Washington, DC: World Peace Foundation and Brookings Institution Press, pp. 137–54.

— (2009) 'China's new risk model for capital investment in Africa', *China Business Frontier*, Stellenbosch, August, pp. 1–4.

De Blij, H. (2012) *Why Geography Matters: More than Ever!*, Oxford and New York: Oxford University Press.

De Janvry, A. (1981) *The Agrarian Question and Reformism in Latin America*, Berkeley: University of California Press.

De Schutter, O. (2011) 'How not to think of land-grabbing: three critiques of large-scale investments in farmland', *Journal of Peasant Studies*, 38(2): 249–79.

Demmissie, S. T. (2011) 'Meles Zenawi's

land lease and famine in Ethiopia', Ethiopian American Information Centre, farmlandgrab.org/post/print/19037.

Denning, G. et al. (2009) 'Input subsidies to improve smallholder maize productivity in Malawi: toward an African Green Revolution', *Plos Biology*, 7(1): 2–10.

Desai, A., B. Maharaj, A. Desai and P. Bond (2010) 'Introduction: Poverty eradication as Holy Grail', in B. Maharaj, A. Desai, A. and P. Bond (eds), *Zuma's Own Goal: Losing South Africa's War on Poverty*, Trenton, NJ: Africa World Press and South Africa Netherlands Research Programme in Alternatives in Development, pp. 1–37.

Deutsche Welthungerhilfe, International Food Policy Research Institute and Concern Worldwide (2011) *Global Hunger Index: The challenge of hunger: Taming price spikes and excessive food price volatility*, Bonn/Washington, DC/Dublin: Welthungerhilfe/International Food Policy Research Institute/Concern Worldwide.

Djité, P. G. (2008) *The Sociolinguistics of Development in Africa*, Clevedon, Buffalo, NY: Multilingual Matters.

Doelling, R. (2008) 'Brazil's contemporary foreign policy towards Africa', *Journal of International Relations*, 10: 5–11.

Dowling, M. J., W. D. Roering, B. A. Carlin and J. Wisnieski (1996) 'Multifaceted relationships under coopetition – description and theory', *Journal of Management Inquiry*, 5(2): 155–67.

DTI (Department of Trade and Industry) (2010) Capital Projects Feasibility Programme, www.thedti.gov.za.

Duncan, J. (2011) 'The print media transformation dilemma', in J. Daniel, P. Naidoo, D. Pillay and R. Southall (eds), *New South African Review 2: New Paths, Old Compromises?*, Johannesburg: University of Witswatersrand Press.

Economist (2009) 'An (iron) fistful of help: China, Iran, Russia and Venezuela have been doling out largesse. Should Western democracies be worried?', *The Economist*, 4 June.

— (2010a) 'Rethinking the "third world": seeing the world differently', *The Economist*, 12 June, pp. 68–9.

— (2010b) 'Brazil's foreign aid programme: speak softly and carry a blank cheque', *The Economist*, 15 July, www.economist.com/node/16592455.

— (2010c) 'Riots in Mozambique: the angry poor', *The Economist*, 9 September, www.economist.com/node/16996835/print.

Economist Intelligence Unit (2005) *Country Report June 2005: Zimbabwe*, London: EIU.

Edinger, H. (n.d.) *BRICs in Africa*, Johannesburg: Frontier Advisory.

England, A. (2011) 'Julius Malema, the Stock Exchange and black share ownership', blogs.ft.com/beyond-brics/2011/10/28/malema-the-stock-exchange-and-black-share-ownership.

Esping-Andersen, G. (1990) *The Three Worlds of Welfare Capitalism*, Cambridge: Polity.

Evans, P. B. (1995) *Embedded Autonomy: States and Industrial Transformation*, Princeton Chapterbacks, Princeton, NJ: Princeton University Press.

Falk, R. A. (1995) *On Humane Governance: Toward a New Global Politics*, World order models project report of the Global Civilization Initiative, University Park: Pennsylvania State University Press.

Farani, M. (2011) in Chatham House (eds), *Brazil's Global Development Agenda*, www.chathamhouse.org/sites/default/files/271011summry.pdf.

Fengler, W. and H. J. Kharas (2010) *Delivering Aid Differently: Lessons from the Field*, Washington, DC: Brookings Institution Press.

Ferguson, J. (1990) *The Anti-Politics Machine: 'Development,' Depoliticization, and Bureaucratic Power in Lesotho*, Minneapolis: University of Minnesota Press.

— (1999) *Expectations of Modernity: Myths and Meanings of Urban Life on the Zambian Copperbelt*, Berkeley, CA, and London: University of California Press.

— (2006) *Global Shadows: Africa in the Neoliberal World Order*, Durham, NC: Duke University Press.

Fidan, H. and B. Aras (2010) 'The return of Russia–Africa relations', *bilig*, 52: 47–68.

Filavotova, I. (2009) 'Russia's plans for Africa: Dmitry Medvedev's visit to Africa this week is Russia's latest attempt to shift the balance of power away from the West', *Guardian*, www.guardian.co.uk.

fin24 (2012) 'Mozambique slams foreign mining firms', 2 February, www.fin24.com/Companies/Mining/Mozambique-slams-foreign-mining-firms-20120202.

Finon, D. (2007) 'Russia and the "Gas-OPEC". Real or perceived threat?', *Russie.Nei.Visions*, 24, Russia/NIS Center.

Flemes, D. (2009) 'Brazilian foreign policy in the changing world order', *South African Journal of International Affairs*, 16(2): 161–82.

Forbes (2011a) 'Africa's richest women', www.forbes.com/fdc/welcome_mjx.shtml.

— (2011b) 'Vladimir Putin', www/forbes.com.

Fraser, A. (2010) 'Introduction', in A. Fraser and M. Larmer (eds), *Zambia, Mining and Neoliberalism: Boom and Bust on the Globalized Copperbelt*, Basingstoke and New York: Palgrave Macmillan.

Fraser, A. and M. Larmer (2010) *Zambia, Mining, and Neoliberalism: Boom and Bust on the Globalized Copperbelt*, New York: Palgrave Macmillan.

Freedom House (various) *Freedom in the World*, Washington, DC: Freedom House.

— (2012) *Freedom in the World in 2012*, www.freedomhouse.org/report/freedom-world/freedom-world-2012.

Frobel, F., J. Heinrichs and O. Kreye (1980) *The New International Division of Labour: Structural Unemployment in Industrialised Countries and Industrialisation in Developing Countries*, Cambridge and New York: Cambridge University Press.

Fundação Dom Cabral and the Columbia Programme on International Investment (2007) 'Brazil's multinationals take off', New York: Fundação Dom Cabral and the Columbia Programme on International Investment.

Gabueuv, A. (2011) 'Russia in Africa: an alternative to China's investment monopoly', *Worldcrunch*, worldcrunch.com/russia-africa-alternative-chinas-investment-monopoly/4335.

Gadgil, M. and R. Guha (1995) *Ecology and Equity: The use and abuse of nature in contemporary India*, London and New York: Routledge.

Gebremedhin, K. (2011) 'African land grab: what Indian companies do in Ethiopia is what they are not allowed to do in India', www.countercurrents.org/goi201211.htm.

German, L., G. Schoneveld and E. Mwangi (2011) 'Processes of large-scale land acquisitions by investors: case studies from sub-Saharan Africa', Occasional paper, CIFOR, www.cifor.org/publications/pdf_files/OccPapers/OP-68.pdf.

Geromel, R. (2011) 'Lula in Guinea Conarky to support Vale', *Brazil Global*, brazilglobal.net.

Ghosh, J. (2011) '"Landgrab" overseas', International Development Economics Associates, www.networkideas.org/news/sep2011/news07_Global_Farmland.htm.

Gibbon, P. (1996) 'Structural adjustment and structural change in sub-Saharan Africa: some provisional conclusions', *Development and Change*, 27(4): 751–84.

Gibbon, P., Y. Bangura and A. Ofstad (1992) *Authoritarianism, Democracy, and Adjustment: The Politics of Economic Reform in Africa*, Uppsala: Nordiska Afrikainstitutet.

Gill, B. and J. Reilly (2007) 'The tenuous hold of China Inc. in Africa', *Washington Quarterly*, 30(3): 37–52.

Gill, S. (2003) *Power and Resistance in the New World Order*, London and New York: Palgrave Macmillan.

— (2008) *Power and Resistance in the New World Order*, 2nd edn, fully revised and updated, Basingstoke and New York: Palgrave Macmillan.

Gillwald, A. and C. Stork (2008) 'Towards evidence-based ICT policy and regulation: ICT access and usage in Africa', www.researchictafrica.net.

Gilroy, P. (1993) *The Black Atlantic: Modernity and Double Consciousness*, Cambridge, MA: Harvard University Press.

Glassman, J. (1999) 'State power beyond the "territorial trap": the internationalization of the state', *Political Geography*, 18(28): 669–96.

GoI Monitor (Government of India) (2011) 'Land grab in Africa, brought to you by India', *Government of India Monitor*, www.goimonitor.com/story/land-grab-africa-brought-you-india.

Gonzales-Vicente, R. (2011) 'The internationalization of the Chinese state', *Political Geography*, 30: 402–11.

Government of Brazil (2013) *The Brazilian Energy Matrix*, www.brasil.gov.br/energia-en/energy-matrix/the-brazilian-energy-matrix/br_model1?set_language=en.

Gray, P. (n.d.) 'The emerging powers and the changing landscape of foreign aid and development cooperation: public perceptions of development cooperation', Geography Dept, University of Cambridge.

— (2011) 'Looking "The Gift" in the mouth', *Anthropology*, 27(2): 5–8.

Greider, W. and K. Rapoza (2003) 'Lula raises the stakes', *The Nation*, www.thenation.com/print/article/lula-raises-stakes.

Gupta, S., C. Pattillo and S. Wagh (2007) 'Impact of remittances on poverty and financial development in sub-Saharan Africa', Working Chapter 07/38, International Monetary Fund.

Gurara, D. and D. Birhanu (2012) 'Large-scale land acquisitions in Africa', *Africa Economic Brief*, 3(5).

Haglund, D. (2008) 'Regulating FDI in weak African states: a case study of Chinese copper mining in Zambia', *Journal of Modern African Studies*, 46(4): 547–75.

— (2009) 'In it for the long term? Governance and learning among Chinese investors in Zambia's copper sector', *China Quarterly*, 199: 627–46.

Hall, R. B. and T. J. Biersteker (eds) (2002) *The Emergence of Private Authority in Global Governance*, Cambridge and New York: Cambridge University Press.

Halper, S. A. (2010) *The Beijing Consensus: How China's Authoritarian Model Will Dominate the Twenty-first Century*, New York: Basic Books.

Hampwaye, G. (2008) 'Decentralisation, local economic development and urban agriculture in Zambia', PhD thesis, University of the Witswatersrand, Johannesburg.

Hampwaye, G. and C. Rogerson (2010) 'Economic restructuring in the Zambian Copperbelt: local responses in Ndola', *Urban Forum*, 21(4): 387–403.

Hanlon, J. (1996) *Peace without Profit: How the IMF Blocks Rebuilding in Mozambique*, Portsmouth, NH: Heinemann.

Harris, N. (1986) *The End of the Third World: Newly Industrializing Countries and the Decline of an Ideology*, London: I. B. Tauris.

Harrison, G. (2004) *The World Bank and Africa: The Construction of Governance States*, London and New York: Routledge.

— (2005) *The World Bank and Africa: The Construction of Governance States*, London: Routledge.

Hart-Landsberg, M. and P. Burkett (2005) *China and Socialism: Market Reforms and Class Struggle*, New York: Monthly Review Press.

Harvey, D. (1982) *The Limits to Capital*, Oxford: Basil Blackwell.

— (2003) *The New Imperialism*, Oxford and New York: Oxford University Press.

— (2005) *A Brief History of Neoliberalism*, Oxford and New York: Oxford University Press.

— (2011) *The Enigma of Capital*, London: Profile Books.

Hassan, F. (2002) *Lesotho: Development in a Challenging Environment*, Abidjan and Washington, DC: African Development Bank and World Bank.

Hausmann, R. and M. Andrews (2009) 'Why we still believe exports for jobs will lead to shared growth: a response to Fine's "Harvard Group shores up shoddy governance"', *Transformation*, 69: 31–65.

Havenevik, K. et al. (2008) 'African agriculture and the World Bank: development or impoverishment?', Policy Dialogue no. 1, Nordic Africa Institute.

He Wenping (2011) 'When BRIC becomes BRICS: the tightening relations between South Africa and China' *East Asia Forum*, www.eastasiaforum. org/2011/03/03/when-bric-becomes-brics-the-tightening-relations-between-south-africa-and-china/ print/.

Heilbrunn, J. (2012) 'Will Romney discover his inner Nixon?', *Foreign Policy*, www.foreignpolicy.com/articles/2012/08/27/will_romney_discover_his_inner_nixon?page=full.

Henderson, J. (1993) 'The role of the state in economic transformation', in C. J. Dixon and D. W. Drakakis-Smith (eds), *Economic and Social Development in Pacific Asia*, London: Routledge.

Hentz, J. J. (2005) *South Africa and the Logic of Regional Cooperation*, Bloomington: Indiana University Press.

— (2008) 'South Africa and the "Three Level Game": globalisation, regionalism and domestic politics', *Commonwealth and Comparative Politics*, 46(4): 490–515.

Herbst, J. and G. Mills (2009) 'Commodity flux and China's Africa strategy', *China Brief: A Journal of Analysis and Information*, X(2): 4–6.

Herskovitz, J. (2010) 'South Africa, not just another BRIC in the wall', Reuters, www.reuters.com/assets/print?aid+USLN6BT00820101230.

Hill, R. (2008) 'Introduction: Perspectives on Putin', *Journal of Communist Studies and Transition Politics*, 24(4): 473–9.

Hoogveen, J. and B. Ozler (2005) 'Not separate, not equal: poverty and inequality in post-apartheid South

Africa', William Davidson Institute Working Chapter, Ann Arbor, MI.

Hu, S. and H. Wei (2011) 'China's harsh squeeze in Zambia's Copper Belt', CaixinOnline, 11 October, english. caixinc.com/2011-11-10-100324752. html.

Hudson, J. (2007) 'South Africa's economic expansion into Africa: neocolonialism or development?', in A. Adebajo, A. Adedeji and C. Landsberg (eds), *South Africa in Africa: The Post-Apartheid Era*, Durban: University of KwaZulu-Natal Press.

IMF (International Monetary Fund) (2009) *Direction of Trade Statistics*, www.imf.org/external/data.htm.

— (2011) 'Data', www.imf.org.

International Movement of People Affected by Vale (2012) 'The Vale 2012 unsustainability report', www.usw.ca/workplace/campaigns/news?id=0035.

International Policy Centre for Inclusive Growth (2009) 'Brazil and Africa newsletter', www.ipc-undp.org/pub/IPCNewsletter6.pdf, accessed 11 July 2012.

International Resource Journal (n.d.) 'Talking Tete – Mozambique's new mining epicentre', *International Resource Journal*, www.international-resourcejournal.com.

Ishiyama, J. (2004) 'The formerly dominant Marxist-Leninist parties in the developing world after the collapse of communism', *Journal of Communist Studies and Transition Politics*, 20(4): 42–60.

ISO (International Standards Organization) (2009) *The ISO Survey – 2008*, www.iso.org/iso/survey2008.pdf.

ITU (International Telecommunications Union) (2009) *Information Society Statistical Profiles 2009: Africa*, Geneva: International Telecommunications Union.

Jacobs, A. (2012) 'Pursuing soft power,

China puts stamp on Africa's news', *New York Times*, 16 August.

Jane's Foreign Report (2002) 'Two geopolitical shifts: i) Oil: Russia's Putin is formulating a long-term strategy', *Jane's Foreign Report*, articles.janes. com/articles/Foreign-Report-2002/Two-geo-political-shifts-i-Oil-Russia-s-Putin-is-formulating-a-long-term-strategy.html.

Jessop, B. (2008) *State Power: A Strategic-Relational Approach*, Cambridge: Polity.

Jessop, B. and N.-L. Sum (2006) *Beyond the Regulation Approach: Putting Capitalist Economies in Their Place*, Cheltenham: Edward Elgar.

JICA (Japanese International Cooperation Agency) (2007) *Summary on the Preliminary Study of the Master Plan Study for Establishing Lusaka South Multi-Facility Economic Zone in the Republic of Zambia*, www.jica. go.jp/english/operations/social_environmental/archive/pro_asia/pdf/zam03_02, accessed 24 August 2010.

Johnson, L. (2012) 'Mitt Romney: Russia is our "number one geopolitical foe"', *Huffington Post*, www.huffingtonpost. com/2012/03/26/mitt-romney-russia- geopolitical-foe_n_1380801. html.

Jok, M. J. (2007) *Sudan: Race, Religion, and Violence*, Oxford: Oneworld.

Jordan, P. (2010) 'A bridge between the Global North and Africa: Putin's Russia and G8 development committments', *African Studies Quarterly*, 11(4): 83–115.

Joseph, R. (1999) 'The reconfiguration of power in late twentieth-century Africa', in R. Joseph (ed.), *State, Conflict and Democracy in Africa*, Boulder, CO: Lynne Rienner.

Jowitt, K. (2008) 'Rus United', *Journal of Communist Studies and Transition Politics*, 24(4): 480–511.

Kahn, M. (2004) *Flight of the Flamingos: A Study on the Mobility of R & D Workers*, Project by the Human Sciences Research Council in partnership with the CSIR for the National Advisory Council on Innovation, Cape Town: Human Sciences Research Council.

Kaplinsky, R., D. McCormick and M. Morris (2010) 'Impacts and challenges of a growing relationship between China and sub-Saharan Africa', in V. Padayachee (ed.), *The Political Economy of Africa*, London and New York: Routledge, pp. 389–409.

Katz, M. (2001) 'Big decisions loom for Russian oil production', www.eura-sianet.org/departments/business/articles/eav112601.shtml.

Kemenade, L. van (2012) 'Rights group: Ethiopia forcibly resettled 70,000', *abc News*, abcnews.go.com/International/rights-group-ethiopia-forcibly-resettled-70000/comments?type= story&id=15376113.

Kennedy, P. M. (2006) 'Russia's plans in Africa', www.inosmi.ru/translation/225318.html.

Kenny, B. and C. Mather (2008) 'Milking the region? South African capital and Zambia's dairy industry', *African Sociological Review*, 12(1): 55–66.

Kiely, R. (2005) *Empire in the Age of Globalisation: US Hegemony and Neoliberal Disorder*, London: Pluto.

— (2008) 'Poverty's fall/China's rise: global convergence or new forms of uneven development?', *Journal of Contemporary Asia*, 38(3): 353–72.

Kim, S. and B. Russett (1996) 'The new politics of voting alignments in the United Nations General Assembly', *International Organization*, 50(4): 629–52.

Kimmage, D. (2009) 'Russia: selective capitalism and kleptocracy', in *Undermining Democracy: 21st Century Authoritarians*, Washington, DC: Freedom House.

Kinch, D. (2012) 'Brazil's PTG Pactual bank creates $1 B private equity fund focused on Africa', online.wsj.com/article/BT-CO-20120503-717202.html, accessed 9 July 2012.

Klare, M. T. (2008) *Rising Powers, Shrinking Planet: How Scarce Energy is Creating a New World Order*, Richmond: Oneworld.

Klomegah, K. (2008) 'A fresh call to review Russia's policy towards Africa', *Modern Ghana News*, www.modernghana.com/news/168277/1/a-fresh-call-to-review-russias-policy-towards-afri.html.

Kragelund, P. (2009a) '"Knocking on a wide-open door": Chinese investments in Africa', *Review of African Political Economy*, 122: 479–97.

— (2009b) 'Part of the disease or part of the cure? Chinese investments in the Zambian mining and construction sectors', *European Journal of Development Research*, 21: 644–61.

— (2009c) 'Bringing indigenous ownership back to the private sector: Chinese investments, populist discourses and contemporary policy making in Zambia', Paper presented at the 52nd Annual Meeting of the African Studies Association (USA), New Orleans.

Kragelund, P. and G. Hampwaye (2012) 'Seeking markets and resources: state-driven Chinese and Indian investments in Zambia', *International Journal of Technology and Globalisation*, 6(4): 352–68.

Kramer, A. (2008) 'Putin's criticism puts $6 billion hole in a company', *New York Times*, 26 July.

Kramer, A. and D. Herszenhorn (2012) 'Midas touch in St Petersburg: friends of Putin glow brightly',

New York Times, www.nytimes.com/2012/03/02/world/europe/ties-to-vladimir-putin-generate-fabulous-wealth-for-a-select-few-in-russia.html?pagewanted=all.

Krasner, S. D. (1985) *Structural Conflict: The Third World against Global Liberalism*, Berkeley and London: University of California Press.

Kraxberger, B. M. (2005) 'The United States and Africa: shifting geopolitics in an "age of terror"', *Africa Today*, 52(1): 47–68.

Laing, A. (2010) 'Zambian miners shot by Chinese managers', *Telegraph*, London, 19 October.

Lamb, H. (1948) *The March of Muscovy; Ivan the Terrible and the Growth of the Russian Empire, 1400–1648*, New York: Doubleday.

Landsberg, C. (2002) 'The impossible neutrality: South Africa's policy in the Congo war', in J. Clark (ed.), *The African Stakes of the Congo War*, Basingstoke and New York: Palgrave Macmillan, pp. 169–84.

Lapeyre, R. (2011) 'The tourism global commodity chain: industry concentration and its impacts on transformation', *Tourism Review International*, 15: 63–75.

Larson, D. W. and A. Shevchenko (2010) 'Status seekers: Chinese and Russian responses to US primacy', *International Security*, 34(4): 63–96.

Lavrov, S. (2012) 'On the right side of history', *Huffington Post*, www.huffingtonpost.co.uk/sergei-lavrov/russia-syria-on-the-right-side-of-history_b_1596400.html.

Lee, M. (2006) 'The 21st century scramble for Africa', *Journal of Contemporary African Studies*, 24(3): 303–29.

Lewis, M. (2011a) 'In Africa, Brazil takes a different track', Reuters Special Report, graphics.thomsonreuters.com/specials/Brazil%20in%20Africa.pdf.

— (2011b) *Boomerang: The Meltdown Tour*, London: Allen Lane.

Lim, K. F. (2010) 'On China's growing geo-economic influence and the evolution of variegated capitalism', *Geoforum*, 41(5): 667–836.

Lineback, N. and M. Lineback Gritzner (2010) *Geography of the Trans-Atlantic Slave Trade*, media.maps101.com/SUB/GITN/ARCHIVES/PDF/1027_020510slavec.pdf.

Lines, T. (2008) *Making Poverty: A History*, London: Zed Books.

Lockwood, M. (2005) *The State They're In: An Agenda for International Action on Poverty in Africa*, Bourton-on-Dunsmore, Warwickshire: ITDG Publishing.

Louis Gates, H. (2011) *Black in Latin America*, New York: New York University Press.

Lovejoy, P. E. (2000) *Transformations in Slavery: A History of Slavery in Africa*, 2nd edn, Cambridge: Cambridge University Press.

Low, S. M. and D. Lawrence-Zúniga (2003) *The Anthropology of Space and Place: Locating Culture*, Malden, MA, and Oxford: Blackwell.

Lungu, J. and C. Mulenga (2005) *Corporate Social Responsibility in the Extractive Industry in Zambia*, Ndola: Mission Press.

Lusaka Times (2009) 'Zambia: China gives Zambia loan for constructing Ndola Stadium', www.lusakatime.com/2009/03/14/china-gives-zambia-loan-for-constructing-ndola.

— (2010) 'Zambia: Govt to address Collum Coal mine woes', www.lusakatimes.com/2010/10/22/govt-address-collum-coal-woes/.

Macauhub (2013) 'Trade between China and Mozambique up 42% from January to November 2012', www.macauhub.com.mo.

Maharaj, B., A. Desai, A. and P. Bond

(eds) (2010) *Zuma's Own Goal: Losing South Africa's War on Poverty*, Trenton, NJ: Africa World Press and South Africa Netherlands Research Programme in Alternatives in Development.

Manby, B. (2009) *Struggles for Citizenship in Africa*, London: Zed Books.

Mankoff, J. (2009) *Russian Foreign Policy: The Return of Great Power Politics*, Lanham, MD: Rowan and Littlefield.

Mann, M. (1986) *The Sources of Social Power*, Cambridge: Cambridge University Press.

Manning, B. (1977) 'The Congress, the Executive and intermetic affairs: three proposals', *Foreign Affairs*, January, pp. 306–24.

Marais, H. (2010) *South Africa Pushed to the Limit: The Political Economy of Change*, Claremont, Cape Town: UCT Press.

Marques, R. M. and A. Mendes (2006) 'The social in Lula's government: building a new populism in the time of the application of the neoliberal agenda', *Journal of Political Economy*, 26(1): 58–74.

Martin, W. (2008) 'South Africa's subimperial futures: Washington Consensus, Bandung Consensus, or Peoples' Consensus', *African Sociological Review*, 12(1): 124–34.

Martinez, O. (1999) *Neoliberalism in Crisis*, Havana: José Martí.

Martins, T. (n.d.) 'Everything in the right place, at the right time', www.odebrechtonline.com.br/materias/01701-01800/1722/.

Matenga, C. (2009) 'The impact of global financial crisis on job losses and conditions of work in the mining sector in Zambia', Mimeo, Lusaka: International Labour Organization.

Matondi, P. (2011) 'Agro-investments in Zimbabwe at a time of redis-tributive land reforms', in P. Matondi, K. Havenevik and A. Beyene (eds), *Biofuels, Land Grabbing and Food Security in Africa*, London: Zed Books, pp. 134–58.

Matondi, P., K. Havenevik and A. Beyene (2011) 'Introduction: Biofuels, land grabbing and food security in Africa', in P. Matondi, K. Havenevik and A. Beyene (eds), *Biofuels, Land Grabbing and Food Security in Africa*, London: Zed Books, pp. 1–20.

Mawdsley, E. (2012) *From Recipients to Donors: Emerging Powers and the Changing Development Landscape*, London: Zed Books.

Mawdsley, E. and G. McCann (2011) *India in Africa: Changing Geographies of Power*, Oxford: Pambazuka.

Mbaye, S. (2010) 'Matching China's activities with Africa's needs', in A. Harneit-Sievers, S. Marks and S. Naidu (eds), *Chinese and African Perspectives on China in Africa*, Cape Town, Nairobi, Dakar and Oxford: Pambazuka Press, pp. 39–54.

Mbeki, M. and J. Rossouw (2010) 'South Africa, time for change', mondiplo.com/blogs/south-africa-time-for-change.

McCulloch, N. and A. Sumner (2009) 'Will the global financial crisis change the development paradigm', www.eadi.org.

McGrath, S. (2013) 'Fuelling global production networks with slave labour? Migrant sugar cane workers in the Brazilian ethanol GPN', *Geoforum*, 44: 32–43.

McGreal, C. (2007) 'Thanks China, now go home: buy-up of Zambia revives old colonial fears', *Guardian*, 5 February, www.guardian.co.uk/world/2007/feb/05/china.chrismcgreal.

McMichael, P. (1997) 'Rethinking globalisation: the agrarian question revisited', *Review of International Political Economy*, 4(4): 630–62.

Media Development and Diversity Agency (2009) 'Trends of ownership and control of media in South Africa', www.mdda.org.za/trends%20of%20 ownership%20and%20control%20 of%20media%20in%20south%20 africa%20-%20over%203.3%20%20 final%20-%2015%20june%202009. pdf.

Meinzen-Dick, R. (2010) 'Overview of "land grabs": global trends, categories, outcomes', Regional workshop on the commercializa-tion of land and 'land grabbing' in southern Africa, Clara Anna Fontein Game Reserve and Country Lodge, Cape Town.

Meles, Z. (2011) 'States and markets: neoliberal limitations and the case for a developmental state', in A. Noman, K. Botchwey, H. Stein, and J. E. Stiglitz (eds), *Good Growth and Governance in Africa: Rethinking Development Strategies* (Initiative for Policy Dialogue), Oxford and New York: Oxford University Press, pp. 140–74.

Meredith, M. (2005) *The State of Africa: A History of Fifty Years of Indepen-dence*, London: Free Press.

Michel, S. and M. Beuret (2009) *China Safari: On the Trail of China's Expan-sion in Africa*, New York: Nation Books.

Midford, P. and I. Soysa (2012) 'Enter the dragon! An empirical analysis of Chinese versus US arms transfers to autocrats and violators of human rights, 1989–2006', *International Studies Quarterly*, 56(4): 843–56.

Milanovic, B. (2011) 'More or less income: inequality has risen over the past quarter-century instead of falling as expected', *Finance and Development*, 48(3), www.imf.org/
external/pubs/ft/fandd/2011/09/ milanovic.htm.

Miller, D. (2003) 'Malling or mauling Africa', *South African Labour Bulletin*, 27(1).

— (2005) 'New regional imaginaries in post-apartheid southern Africa – retail workers at a shopping mall in Zambia', *Journal of Southern African Studies*, 31(1): 117–45.

Miller, D., O. Oloyede and R. Saunders (2008) 'South African corporations and post-apartheid expansion in Africa', *African Sociological Review*, 12(1): 1–19.

Mittelman, J. H. (2000) *The Globalisa-tion Syndrome: Transformation and Resistance*, Princeton, NJ: Princeton University Press.

mobileworld (2012) 'MTN reaches over 170 million subscribers', www. mobileworldmag.com/mtn-reaches-over-170-million-subscribers.html.

Moisi, D. (2009) *The Geopolitics of Emotion: How Cultures of Fear, Humiliation, and Hope are Reshaping the World*, New York: Doubleday.

Monama, M. (2009) 'Black CEOs thin on ground', www.fin24.com/ Business/Black-CEOs-thin-on-ground-20090621.

Monson, J. (2009) *Africa's Freedom Railway: How a Chinese Development Project Changed Lives and Livelihoods in Tanzania*, Bloomington: Indiana University Press.

Mosley, L. (2005) 'Globalisation and the state: still room to move?', *New Political Economy*, 10(3): 355–62.

Moulds, J. (2012) 'China's economy to overtake US in next four years, says OECD', *Guardian*, 9 November, www.guardian.co.uk/business/2012/ nov/09/china-overtake-us-four-years-oecd.

Moyo, D. (2009) *Dead Aid: Why Aid is Not Working and How There is a*

Better Way for Africa, New York: Farrar, Straus and Giroux.

— (2012) *Winner Take All: China's Race for Resources and What It Means for Us*, London: Allen Lane.

MTN (2009) *2008 Annual Report*, www.mtn-investor.com/mtn_aro8/.

Murphy, R. (2012) *Inside Irish Aid: The Impulse to Help*, Dublin: Liffey Press.

Murray Li, T. (2011) 'Centering labor in the land grab debate', *Journal of Peasant Studies*, 38(2): 281–98.

Mutati, F. (2009) 'Statement on the MFEZ development by the Minister of Commerce, Trade and Industry, the Honorable Felix Mutati', 18 February, www.scribd.com.

Mutesa, F. (2010) 'China and Zambia: between development and politics', in F. Cheru and C. Obi (eds), *The Rise of China and India in Africa*, Uppsala and London: Nordiska Afrikainstitutet and Zed Books, pp. 167–80.

Naidu, S. (2009) 'India's engagements in Africa: self-interest or mutual partnership?', in R. Southall and H. Melber (eds), *A New Scramble for Africa? Imperialism, Investment and Development*, Durban: University of KwaZulu-Natal Press.

— (2010) 'India's African relations: in the shadow of China?', in F. Cheru and C. Obi (eds), *The Rise of China and India in Africa*, Uppsala and London: Nordiska Afrikainstitutet and Zed Books.

— (2011) 'Upping the ante in Africa: India's increasing footprint across the continent', in E. Mawdsley and G. McCann (eds), *India in Africa: Changing geographies of power*, Cape Town: Pambazuka Press, pp. 48–67.

Nally, D. (2011a) 'Against food security', Paper presented at 'Geopolitics, Ireland and the new world order', National University of Ireland, Maynooth, Co. Kildare.

— (2011b) 'The biopolitics of food provisioning', *Transactions of the Institute of British Geographers*, 36(1): 37–53.

— (2011c) *Human Encumbrances: Political Violence and the Great Irish Famine*, Notre Dame, IN: University of Notre Dame Press.

Namusa, K. (2012) 'Zambia: China happy with nation's economic results', *Times of Zambia*, 29 December, allafrica.com/stories/201212310618.html.

National Council for Construction (2009) 'Registered contractors and gradings', Unpublished chapter, Lusaka: National Council for Construction.

Nederveen Pieterse, J. (2010) *Development Theory: Deconstructions/Reconstructions*, 2nd edn, London: Sage.

Negi, R. (2008) 'Beyond the "Chinese Scramble": the political economy of anti-China sentiment in Zambia', *African Geographical Review*, 27: 41–63.

Nel, P. (2010) 'Redistribution and recognition: what emerging regional powers want', *Review of International Studies*, 36(4): 951–74.

NEPAD (2001) *The New Partnership for Africa's Development*, www.dfa.gov.za/au.nepad/nepad.pdf.

— (2010) 'President Zuma reiterates commitment to NEPAD', www.nepad.org.

Ness, B. et al. (2009) 'The African landgrab: creating equitable governance strategies through Codes-of-Conduct and certification schemes', www.earthsystemgovernance.org/ac2009/chapters/AC2009-0294.pdf.

Neumann, I. (2003) 'A region building approach', in F. Söderbaum and T. Shaw (eds), *Theories of the New Regionalism*, Basingstoke and New York: Palgrave.

New York Times (2012) 'Five years later, some countries still lag', www.

nytimes.com/interactive/2012/12/28/ Five-Years-Later-Some-Countries-Still-Lag.

Nolan, P. (2009) *Crossroads: The End of Wild Capitalism and the Future of Humanity*, London: Marshall Cavendish Business.

Noury, V. (2012) 'Africa–India: a partnership made in heaven', *African Business*, 382: 35–7.

Numusa, K. (2012) 'Zambia: China happy with nation's economic results', *Times of Zambia*, allafrica.com/stories/printable/201212310618.html.

Nye, J. S. (2004) *Soft Power: The Means to Success in World Politics*, New York/Oxford: Public Affairs/Oxford Publicity Partnership (distributor).

O'Connor, M. (1994) *Is Capitalism Sustainable?: Political Economy and the Politics of Ecology*, New York: Guilford Press.

O'Neill, J. (2011) *The Growth Map: Economic Opportunity in the BRICs and Beyond*, London: Portfolio Penguin.

OECD (Organisation for Economic Co-operation and Development) (2008) 'China's outward foreign direct investment', *OECD Investment News*, 6: 1–8.

— (2009) *Factbook 2009*, www.oecd-ilibrary.org/economics/oecd-factbook-2009_factbook-2009-en.

— (2011) 'Aid for trade: case story Brazil', www.oecd.org/dataoecd/61/18/47699046.pdf.

Ogier, T. (2012) 'Beyond trade; Brazil's aid to Africa', *Latin Business Chronicle*, www.latinbusinesschronicle.com.

Oil and Gas Journal (2003) 'Talisman marks end of era with completion of Sudan sale', *Oil and Gas Journal*, 101(14).

Okumu, W. (2002) *The African Renaissance: History, Significance and Strategy*, Trenton, NJ: Africa World Press.

Oliveira Ribeiro, C. (2009) 'Brazil's new African policy', *World Affairs: The Journal of International Issues*, 13(1): 84–93.

Ombok, E. (2011) 'Russia's Renaissance Capital plans expansion in East Africa as IPOs rise', *Bloomberg*, www.bloomberg.com/news/2011-08-19/renaissance-capital-plans-rwanda-office-as-initial-public-offerings-grow.html.

Ong, A. (2000) 'Graduated sovereignty in South-East Asia', *Theory Culture and Society*, 17(4): 55–75.

Osumare, H. (2012) *The Hiplife in Ghana: West African Indigenization of Hip-Hop*, Basingstoke and New York: Palgrave Macmillan.

Oxford Analytica (2012) 'Russia and foreign aid ambitions outpace mixed results', www.oxan.com/display.aspx?ItemID=ES175339.

Palloti, A. (2004) 'SADC: a development community without a development policy?', *Review of African Political Economy*, 101: 513–31.

Palmer, R. (2010) 'Would Cecil Rhodes have signed a Code of Conduct? Reflections on global land grabbing and land rights in Africa', Paper presented at the African Studies Association of the UK biennial conference, Oxford.

Paquet, G. (1996) *The New Geogovernance: a Baroque Approach*, Ottawa: University of Ottawa Press.

Parenti, C. (2011) *Tropic of Chaos: Climate Change and the New Geography of Violence*, New York: Nation Books.

Parfitt, T. (2012) 'Vladimir Putin: the Russian president's "life of four yachts and 58 aircraft"', *Daily Telegraph*, www.telegraph.co.uk/news/worldnews/vladimir-putin/9503469/Vladimir-Putin-the-Russian-presidents-life-of-four-yachts-and-58-aircraft.html.

Patey, L. A. (2011) 'India in Sudan: troubles in an African "oil paradise"', in D. Large and L. A. Patey (eds), *Sudan Looks East: China, India and the politics of Asian alternatives*, New York: James Currey, pp. 87–101.

Paul, T. V. (2005) 'Soft balancing in the age of US primacy', *International Security*, 30(1): 46–71.

Pearce, F. (2012) *The Landgrabbers: The Fight over Who Owns the Earth*, London: Transworld.

Peck, J. (2004) 'Geography and public policy: constructions of neoliberalism', *Progress in Human Geography*, 28(3): 392–405.

Peiffer, C. and P. Englebert (2012) 'Extraversion, vulnerability to donors, and political liberalization in Africa', *African Affairs*, 111(444): 355–78.

People's Daily Online (2010) 'South Africa's entry into BRIC to reshape world economy', *People's Daily Online*, english.peopledaily.com.cn/90001/90780/91421/7247209.html.

Pham, P. (2008) 'The Russian bear returns to Africa', *AUMonitor*, www.pambazuka.org/aumonitor/comments/1696/.

Phillips, N. (1998) 'Globalisation and the "paradox of state power": perspectives from Latin America', Centre for the Study of Globalisation and Regionalisation Working Paper no. 16/98, Coventry.

Polanyi, K. (1944) *The Great Transformation*, New York and Toronto: Farrar & Rinehart.

Prates, D. M. and L. M. Paulani (2007) 'The financial globalisation of Brazil under Lula', *Monthly Review*, www.monthlyreview.org.

Provost, C. (2011) 'The rebirth of Russian foreign aid', *Guardian*, www.guardian.co.uk/global-development/2011/may/25/russia-foreign-aid-report-influence-image.

— (2012) 'International land deals: who is investing where – get the data', *Guardian Datablog*, www.guardian.co.uk.

Putin, V. (2002) 'President of the Russian Federation Vladimir Putin remarks at press conference following Big Eight Summit, Kananaskis, Canada', www.ln.mid/ru/bl.nsf.

Qi, D., W. Wu and H. Zhang (2000) 'Shareholding structure and corporate performance of partially privatised firms: evidence from listed Chinese companies', *Pacific-Basin Finance Journal*, 8: 587–610.

Radelet, S. C. (2010) *Emerging Africa: How 17 Countries are Leading the Way*, Washington, DC: Center for Global Development/Brookings Institution Press.

Radio Free Europe and Radio Liberty (2009) 'Undermining democracy: twenty first century authoritarians', www.underminingdemocracy.org/execSummary.php.

Rahmato, D. (2011) 'Land to investors: large-scale land transfers in Ethiopia', Addis Ababa.

Raine, S. (2009) *China's African Challenges*, Abingdon and New York: Routledge for the International Institute for Strategic Studies.

Ravenhill, J. (1986) 'The elusiveness of development', in J. Ravenhill (ed.), *Africa in Economic Crisis*, London: Macmillan.

Renaissance Capital (2013) www.rencap.com/ContactUs/ByLocations/?reg=5.

Reuters (2012) 'Zambian miners kill Chinese supervisor and injure another in pay dispute', in.reuters.com/article/2012/08/05/zambia-mines-idINL6E8J511T20120805.

Ritzer, G. (2010) *Globalization: A Basic Text*, Malden, MA: Wiley-Blackwell.

Robertson, C. (2012) *The Fastest Billion: The Story Behind Africa's Economic*

Revolution, London: Renaissance Capital.

Robertson, R. (1997) 'Comments on the "Global Triad" and "Glocalization"' 1997', www2.kokugakuin.ac.jp/ijcc/wp/global/15robertson.html.

Robinson, W. (2002) 'Capitalist globalisation and the transnationalization of the state', in M. Rupert and H. Smith (eds), *Historical Materialism and Globalisation*, London and New York: Routledge.

Rogerson, C. (2005) 'The emergence of tourism-led local development', *Africa Insight*, 35(4): 112–20.

— (2007) 'Reviewing Africa in the global tourism economy', *Development Southern Africa*, 24: 361–79.

Rose, R. (2012) *New Russia Barometer XX. Public Opinion of Vladimir Putin's Return as President*, Glasgow: University of Strathclyde.

Rowden, R. (2011) 'India's role in the new global farmland grab: an examination of the role of the Indian government and Indian companies engaged in overseas agricultural land acquisitions in developing countries', Produced in collaboration with GRAIN and the Economics Research Foundation, www.ifad.org/drd/agriculture/103.htm.

Rugman, J. (2012) 'Africa succumbs to colonial-style land grab', *Channel 4 News*, 7 January, www.channel4.com/news/africa-succumbs-to-colonial-style-land-grab.

Rundell, S. (2010) 'Massive profits follow S Africa's northern invasion', *African Business*, May, pp. 40–4.

Rutland, P. (2008) 'Russia as an energy superpower', *New Political Economy*, 13(2): 203–10.

— (2012) 'Still out in the cold? Russia's place in a globalizing world', *Communist and Post-Communist Studies*, 45(3/4): 343–54.

SABMiller (2013) 'Tanzania Breweries Limited', www.sabmiller.com/index.asp?pageid=1166.

Samatar, A. I. (2004) 'Ethiopian federalism: autonomy versus control in the Somali region', *Third World Quarterly*, 25(6): 1131–54.

Sanchez, D. (2008) 'Transnational telecommunications capital expanding from South Africa into Africa: adapting to African growth and South African transformation demands', *African Sociological Review*, 12(1): 105–23.

SAPA (2012) 'Zuma responds to "tipping point" comment', www.iol.co.za/news/politics/zuma-responds-to-tipping-point-comment-1.1413797.

Saravia, E. (2012) 'Brazil: towards innovation in development cooperation', in S. Chaturvedi, T. Fues and E. Sidiropoulos (eds), *Development Cooperation and Emerging Powers: New Partners or Old Patterns?*, London: Zed Books.

Schmitz, H. and Y. Hewitt (1991) 'Learning to raise infants: a case-study in industrial policy', in C. Colcough and J. Manor (eds), *States or Markets? Neoliberalism and the Development Policy Debate*, Oxford: Oxford University Press.

Schoeman, M. (2007) 'South Africa in Africa: behemoth, hegemon, partner or "just another kid on the block"?', in A. Adebajo, A. Adedeji and C. Landsberg (eds), *South Africa in Africa: The Post-Apartheid Era*, Durban: University of KwaZulu-Natal Press, pp. 92–104.

Schroeder, R. (2008) 'South African capital in the land of Ujamaa: contested terrain in Tanzania', *African Sociological Review*, 12(1): 20–34.

— (2010) 'Tanzanite as conflict gem: certifying a secure commodity chain in Tanzania', *Geoforum*, 41(1): 56–65.

— (2012) *Africa after Apartheid: South Africa, Race and Nation in Tanzania*, Bloomington and Indianapolis: Indiana University Press.

Scott, J. C. (1998) *Seeing Like a State: How Certain Schemes to Improve the Human Condition Have Failed*, New Haven, CT: Yale University Press.

Scott, J., M. vom Hau and D. Hulme (2012) 'Beyond the BRICs: identifying the "Emerging Middle Powers" and understanding their role in global poverty reduction', *European Journal of Development Research*, 24: 187–204.

Seibert, G. (2012) 'Brazil in Africa: ambitions and achievements of an emerging regional power in the political and economic sector', in *Fourth European Conference on African Studies*, Nordic Africa Institute, Uppsala, www.nai.uu.se/ecas-4/panels/1-20/panel-8/Gerhard-Seibert-Full-paper.pdf.

Selvanayagam, R. (2011) 'Brazil's growing economic relationship with Africa', www.brazilinvestmentguide.com/blog/2011/05/brazil%E2%80%99s-growing-economic-relationship-with-africa/.

Sender, J. (1999) 'Africa's economic performance: limitations of the current consensus', *Journal of Economic Perspectives*, 13(3): 89–114.

Sharma, R. (2012) 'Broken BRICs: why the rest stopped rising', *Foreign Affairs*, November/December, www.foreignaffairs.com/articles/138219/ruchir-sharma/broken-brics.

Shaw, M. (2003) 'The state of globalization: towards a theory of state transformation', in N. Brenner, B. Jessop, M. Jones and G. MacLeod (eds), *State/Space: A Reader*, Oxford: Blackwell.

Shaw, T. M., A. F. Cooper and G. T. Chin (2009) 'Emerging powers and Africa: implications for/from global governance?', *Politikon*, 36(1): 27–44.

Shinn, D. H. and J. Eisenman (2012) *China and Africa: A Century of Engagement*, Philadelphia: University of Pennsylvania Press.

Shiva, V. (2007) 'From corporate land grab to land sovereignty', *ZMag*, www.countercurrents.org/shiva 100207.htm.

— (2008) *Soil Not Oil: Environmental Justice in a Time of Climate Crisis*, Cambridge, MA: South End Press.

Shoprite (2003) *Annual Report: Africa Vision*, www.shopriteholdings.co.za/files/1019812640/Investor_Centre_Files/Annual_Reports/Annual%20 Report %202003.pdf.

— (2005) *Annual Report: Proudly South Africa, Proudly African*, www.shoprite holdings.co.za/files/1019812640/Investor_Centre_Files/Annual_Reports/Annual_Report_2005.pdf.

Shubin, V. (2004) 'Russian and Africa: moving in the right direction?', in P. Williams and I. Taylor (eds), *Africa in International Politics: External Involvement on the Continent*, London: Routledge.

— (2010) 'Russia and Africa: coming back?', *Russian Analytical Digest*, 83: 4–7.

Shutt, H. (2009) *The Trouble with Capitalism: An Enquiry into the Causes of Global Economic Failure*, new edn, London: Zed Books.

Sidaway, J. D. (2012) 'Geographies of development: new maps, new visions?', *Professional Geographer*, 64(1): 49–62.

Simonov, K. V. (2006) *E\0307 nergeticheskai\FE20a\FE21 sverkhderzhava*, Moscow: Algoritm.

Sklair, L. (2001) *The Transnational Capitalist Class*, Oxford: Blackwell.

Smith, J. (2010) *Biofuels and the Globalisation of Risk: The biggest change* in *North–South relationships since colonialism?*, London: Zed Books.

Smith, K. (2012) 'South–South cooperation in the 21st century: have pragmatic, exclusive alliances replaced ideological solidarity?', Paper presented to the IPSA conference, 8–12 July, Madrid.

Smith, K., T. Fordelone and F. Zimmermann (2010) 'Beyond the DAC: the welcome role of other providers of development co-operation', www.oecd.org/dataoecd/58/24/45361474.pdf.

Soares de Lima, M. R. and M. Hirst (2006) 'Brazil as an intermediate state and regional power: action, choice and responsibilities', *International Affairs*, 82(1): 21–40.

Söderbaum, F. (2004) *The Political Economy of Regionalism: The Case of Southern Africa*, Basingstoke and New York: Palgrave Macmillan.

Solignac-Lecomte, H. B. (2013) Royal Irish Academy masterclass, Dublin, 16 January.

South African Government News Service (2011) 'South Africa: SA must proceed cautiously with BRIC countries say analysts', 7thspace.com.

South African Reserve Bank (2010) 'International economic relations', www.resbank.co.za/Pages/default.aspx.

Southall, R. and A. Comninos (2009) 'The scramble for Africa and the marginalization of African capitalism', in R. Southall and H. Melber (eds), *A New Scramble for Africa? Imperialism, Investment and Development*, Durban: University of KwaZulu-Natal Press, pp. 357–85.

Southern African Report (2011) 'The ANC, business and the "sins of incumbency"', *Southern African Report*, www.southernafricareport.com/.

Statistics South Africa (2010) 'Data', www.statssa.gov.za/default.asp.

— (2011) *South African Trade by Con-*tinents, www.thedti.gov.za/econdb/raportt/rapcont.html.

Stavrianos, L. (1981) *Global Rift: The Third World Comes of Age*, New York: Morrow.

Stiglitz, J. (2010) Comments on chapter at Beyond the BRICs workshop, 28 June, University of Manchester.

Stockholm International Peace Research Institute (2012) 'Arms transfer database', armstrade.sipri.org/armstrade/page/toplist.php.

Strange, S. (1996) *The Retreat of the State: The Diffusion of Power in the World Economy*, New York: Cambridge University Press.

— (1999) 'The Westfailure system', *Review of International Studies*, 25(3): 345–54.

Sunday Guardian (2012) 'India sets up global aid agency', *Sunday Guardian*, 1 July, www.sunday-guardian.com/news/india-sets-up-global-aid-agency.

Sweig, J. E. (2010) 'A new global player: Brazil's far-flung agenda', *Foreign Affairs*, 89(6), www.foreignaffairs.com/articles/66868/julia-e-sweig/a-new-global-player.

Swyngedouw, E. (1997) 'Neither global nor local: glocalization and the politics of scale', in K. R. Cox (ed.), *Spaces of Globalisation: Reasserting the power of the local*, New York and London: Guilford Press.

Tan-Mullins, M., G. Mohan and M. Power (2010) 'Redefining "aid" in the China–Africa context', *Development and Change*, 41(5): 857–81.

Tavener, B. (2012) 'Brazil's Africa exports show major growth', *Rio Times*, 24 July, riotimesonline.com/brazil-news/rio-business/brazils-africa-exports-show-major-growth/#.

Taylor, I. (2006) *China and Africa: Engagement and Compromise*, Abingdon and New York: Routledge.

— (2009) *China's New Role in Africa*, Boulder, CO: Lynne Rienner.

— (2010) *The International Relations of Sub-Saharan Africa*, New York: Continuum.

— (2011) 'South African "imperialism" in a region lacking regionalism: a critique', *Third World Quarterly*, 32(7): 1233–53.

Taylor, S. D. (2012) *Globalisation and the Cultures of Business in Africa: From Patrimonialism to Profit*, Indianapolis and Bloomington: Indiana University Press.

Theron, M. (2011) 'African trends and transformation: the profiles of sub-Saharan African executive heads of state since independence', Research Paper 17, Developmental Leadership Program, www.dlprog.org.

Thomas, H. (1997) *The Slave Trade: The History of the Atlantic Slave Trade, 1440–1870*, London: Picador.

Tilley, H. (2011) *Africa as a Living Laboratory: Empire, Development, and the Problem of Scientific Knowledge, 1870–1950*, Chicago, IL: University of Chicago Press.

Tleane, C. (2006) *The Great Trek North: The Expansion of South African Media and ICT Companies into the SADC region*, Braamfontein: Freedom of Expression Institute.

Tomson, W. and R. Ahrend (2006) *Realising the Oil Supply Potential of the CIS*, Economics Department Working Chapter, OECD.

Toulmin, C. (2009) *Climate Change in Africa*, London and New York: Zed Books in association with the International African Institute and the Royal African Society.

Transparency International (2006) *Bribe Payer's Index 2006 Analysis Report*, Transparency International.

Trenin, D. (2006) 'Russia leaves the West', *Foreign Affairs*, 85(4), www.foreignaffairs.com/articles/61735/dmitri-trenin/russia-leaves-the-west.

Tull, D. M. (2006) 'China's engagement in Africa: scope, significance and consequences', *Journal of Modern African Studies*, 44(3): 459–79.

UN (2009) 'Africa's cooperation with new and emerging development partners: options for Africa's development', www.un.org/africa/osaa/reports/emerging_economies_2009.pdf, accessed 12 July 2012.

UNCTAD (United Nations Conference on Trade and Development) (2005) *Case Study on Outward Foreign Direct Investment by South African Enterprises*, Chapter produced by Trade and Development Board, Commission on Enterprise, Business Facilitation and Development for Expert Meeting on Enhancing Productive Capacity of Developing Country Firms through Internationalization, Geneva, 5–7 December.

— (2006) *World Investment Report 2006. FDI from Developing and Transition Economies: Implications for Development*, New York and Geneva: UNCTAD.

— (2007) *Asian Foreign Direct Investment in Africa: Towards a New Era of Cooperation among Developing Countries*, New York: United Nations.

— (2009a) *Economic Development in Africa: Strengthening Regional Economic Integration in Africa's Development*, Geneva: UNCTAD.

— (2009b) *World Investment Report 2009*, Geneva: UNCTAD.

— (2010) *Economic Development in Africa Report 2010: South-South Cooperation: Africa and the New Forms of Development Partnership*, Geneva: UNCTAD.

— (2012) *World Investment Report 2012: Towards a New Generation of Investment Policies*, www.unctad-docs.org/

files/UNCTAD-WIR2012-Full-en.pdf, accessed 9 July 2012.

UNDP (2008) 'Cooperation with Brazil–Ghana', www.ipcundp.org/ipc/PageAfrica-Brazil.do?id=11#gana.

— (2012) *Human Development Report*, hdrstats.undp.org/en/countries/profiles/ZAF.html.

United Kingdom Department for International Development (2011) 'Business plan 2011–2015', www.dfid.gov.uk/Documents/DFID-business-plan.pdf.

Urnov, A. (2009) 'Russia and Africa', www.inafran.ru/sites/default/files/page_file/%20%D0%A0%D0%9E%D0%A1%D0%A1%D0%98%D0%AF%20%D0%98%20%D0%90%D0%A4%D0%A0%D0%98%D0%9A%D0%90%D0%90.pdf.

US Commercial Service (2009) 'Doing business in Zambia: a country commercial guide for US companies', zambia.usembassy.gov/root/pdfs/2009ccg.pdf, accessed 17 August 2010.

Van de Walle, N. (2001) *African Economies and the Politics of Permanent Crisis, 1979–1999*, Cambridge: Cambridge University Press.

Vassiliev, A. (2003) *Africka – padcherista globalizatsii* [Africa: a stepchild of globalization], Moscow: Vostochnaya Literatura.

— (2011) 'Russia and Africa: vying for mineral resources', en.rian.ru/valdai_op/20110510/163950350.html.

Vigevani, T. and G. Cepaluni (2009) *Brazilian Foreign Policy in Changing Times: The Quest for Autonomy from Sarney to Lula*, Lanham, MD: Lexington Books.

Visentini, P. F. (2010) 'South–South cooperation, prestige diplomacy or "soft imperialism"? Lula's government Brazil–Africa relations', in D. Rolland and C. Lessa (eds), *Brazil's International Relations: Paths to Power*, Paris: L'Hartmann.

Voice of Russia (2011) 'Russia predicted millionaires boom in 2020', english. ruvr.ru/2011/05/11/50150226.html.

Vom Hau, M., J. Scott and D. Hulme (2012) 'Beyond the BRICs: alternative strategies of influence in the global politics of development: introduction', *European Journal of Development Research*, 24(2): 187–204.

Von Braun, J. and R. Meinzen-Dick (2009) '"Land grabbing" by foreign investors in developing countries: risks and opportunities', International Food Policy Research Institute Policy Brief, www.ifpri.org/sites/default/files/publications/bp013all.pdf.

Wade, R. H. (2011) 'Emerging world order? From multipolarity to multilateralism in the G20, the World Bank, and the IMF', *Politics and Society*, 39(3): 347–77.

Wahome, M. (2012) 'Kenya: bitter beer wars help keep advertising revenues high', *Daily Nation*, 7 February, allafrica.com/stories/printable/201202071016.html.

Walton, J. and D. Seddon (1994) *Free Markets and Food Riots: The Politics of Global Adjustment*, Oxford: Blackwell.

Weir, F. (2010) 'Russia flexes military power with "futuristic" fighter jet', *Christian Science Monitor*, www.csmonitor.com/World/Europe/2010/0129/Russia-flexes-military-power-with-futuristic-fighter-jet.

Weiss, L. (1998) *The Myth of the Powerless State*, Ithaca, NY: Cornell University Press.

Weiss, T. (2010) 'The accelerating biophysical contradictions of industrial capitalist agriculture', *Journal of Agrarian Change*, 10(3): 315–41.

Wendt, A. (1999) *Social Theory of Interna-*

tional Politics, Cambridge: Cambridge University Press.

White, L. (2010) 'Understanding Brazil's new drive for Africa', *South African Journal of International Affairs*, 17(2): 221–42.

Willcox, O. and D. van Seventer (2005) 'Current and potential trade between South Africa and China', in P. Draper and G. Le Pere (eds), *Enter the Dragon: Towards a Free Trade Agreement between China and the Southern African Customs Union*, Midrand and Johannesburg: Institute for Global Dialogue and the South African Institute for International Affairs, pp. 167–220.

Williams, E. (1994) *Capitalism and Slavery*, Chapel Hill: University of North Carolina Press.

Wilson, A. (2012) 'Putin returns, but will Russia revert to "virtual democracy"?', www.opendemocracy. net/od-russia/ andrew-wilson/putin-returns-but-will-russia-revert-to-%E2%80%98virtual-democracy%E2%80%9.

Wilson, D. and R. Purushothaman (2003) 'Dreaming with BRICs: the path to 2050', in *Global Economics Chapter No. 99*, Goldman Sachs.

Wood, E. M. (2003) *Empire of Capital*, London: Verso.

World Bank (2012) 'Data', dataworldbank. org.

— (2013) 'Data', dataworldbank.org.

World Bank and IPEA (2011) *Bridging the Atlantic: Brazil and Sub Saharan Africa, South–South Partnering for Growth*, siteresources.worldbank. org/AFRICAEXT/Resources/africa-brazil-bridging-final.pdf.

World Economic Forum on Africa (2010) 'Case study: Mozambique natural gas project', www.sasol.com/sasol_internet/downloads/WEF_Moz_case_study_1273134130298.pdf.

Xinhua (2003) 'Zambia export processing zone authority starts to operate',

www.highbeam.com/doc/ 1P2-1342 0218.html, accessed 19 October 2010.

— (2010) 'Wen says achieving the MDGs remain long, uphill journey, promises to expand China's foreign aid', english.peopledaily.com. cn/90001/90776/90883/7148297. html, accessed 6 October 2010.

Yates, D. (2012) *The Scramble for African Oil: Oppression, Corruption and War for Control of Africa's Natural Resources*, London: Pluto.

Youde, J. (2007) 'Why look East? Zimbabwean foreign policy and China', *Africa Today*, 53(3): 3–19.

Zambanker Reporter (2008) 'BOC regu-latory capital swells by 1000%', *Zambanker: A Bank of Zambia Journal*, p. 1.

Zenawi, M. (2011) 'States and markets: neoliberal limitations and the case for a developmental state', in A. Noman, K. Botchwey, H. Stein and J. Stiglitz (eds), *Good Growth and Governance in Africa*, Oxford and New York: Oxford University Press, pp. 140–74.

Zoellick, R. (2010) *The End of the Third World? Modernizing Multilateralism for a Multipolar World*, web.world bank.org.

Zoomers, A. (2010) 'Globalisation and the foreignisation of space: seven processes driving the current global land grab', *Journal of Peasant Studies*, 37(2): 429–47.

— (2011) 'Introduction: Rushing for land: equitable and sustainable development in Africa, Asia and Latin America', *Development*, 54(1): 12–20.

Zuma, J. (2010a) 'Zuma calls for action on infrastructure', www. nepad.org/regionalintegrationand infrastructure/ news/1906/zuma-calls-action-infrastructure.

— (2010b) *State of the Nation Address 2010*, www.thepresidency.gov.za/ pebble.asp?relid=11.

INDEX